THE Complete
Student Missions
Handbook

Zondervan/Youth Specialties Books

Adventure Games
Amazing Tension Getters
Called to Care
The Complete Student Missions Handbook
Creative Socials and Special Events
Divorce Recovery for Teenagers
Feeding Your Forgotten Soul (Spiritual Growth for Youth Workers)
Get 'Em Talking
Good Clean Fun
Good Clean Fun, Volume 2
Great Games for 4th–6th Graders (Get 'Em Growing)
Great Ideas for Small Youth Groups
Greatest Skits on Earth
Greatest Skits on Earth, Volume 2
Growing Up in America
High School Ministry
High School TalkSheets
Holiday Ideas for Youth Groups (Revised Edition)
Hot Talks
Ideas for Social Action
Intensive Care: Helping Teenagers in Crisis
Junior High Ministry
Junior High TalkSheets
The Ministry of Nurture
On-Site: 40 On-Location Programs for Youth Groups
Option Plays
Organizing Your Youth Ministry
Play It! Great Games for Groups
Teaching the Bible Creatively
Teaching the Truth about Sex
Tension Getters
Tension Getters II
Unsung Heroes: How to Recruit and Train Volunteer Youth Workers
Up Close and Personal: How to Build Community in Your Youth Group
Youth Specialties Clip Art Book
Youth Specialties Clip Art Book, Volume 2

THE Complete Student Missions Handbook

A step-by-step guide to lead your group out of the classroom and into the field

Ridge Burns
WITH Noel Becchetti

Youth Specialties
Zondervan Publishing House
Grand Rapids, Michigan

THE COMPLETE STUDENT MISSIONS HANDBOOK
Copyright © 1990 by Youth Specialties, Inc.

Youth Specialties Books, 1224 Greenfield Drive, El Cajon, California 92021, are published by Zondervan Publishing House, 1415 Lake Drive, S.E., Grand Rapids, Michigan 49506

Library of Congress Cataloging-in-Publication Data

Burns, Ridge.
    The complete student missions handbook / Ridge Burns with Noel Becchetti.
        p.   cm.
    ISBN 0-310-52851-8
    1. Youth in missionary work. I. Becchetti, Noel, 1955–   .
II. Title.
BV2617.B87   1990
266'.00835—dc20   90-38104
                                                                          CIP

All Scripture quotations, unless otherwise noted, are taken from the *Holy Bible: New International Version* (North American Edition). Copyright © 1973, 1978, 1984 by the International Bible Society. Used by permission of Zondervan Bible Publishers.

Edited by Kathi George
Designed by Blue Water Ink
Cover design and photography by Mark Rayburn

Printed in the United States of America

90 91 92 93 94 95 96 97 98 99 / AK / 10 9 8 7 6 5 4 3 2 1

About the YouthSource™ Publishing Group

YouthSource™ books, tapes, videos, and other resources pool the expertise of three of the finest youth-ministry resource providers in the world:

• **Campus Life Books**—publishers of the award-winning *Campus Life* magazine, who for nearly fifty years have helped high schoolers live Christian lives.

• **Youth Specialties**—serving ministers to middle-school, junior-high, and high-school youth for over twenty years through books, magazines, and training events such as the National Youth Workers Convention.

• **Zondervan Publishing House**—one of the oldest, largest, and most respected evangelical Christian publishers in the world.

Campus Life
465 Gundersen Dr.
Carol Stream, IL 60188
708-260-6200

Youth Specialties
1224 Greenfield Dr.
El Cajon, CA 92021
619-440-2333

Zondervan
1415 Lake Dr., S.E.
Grand Rapids, MI 49506
616-698-6900

To Chuck Wickman, Chris Lyons, and Homer Waisner,
senior pastors of the churches I served.
Their faith in student missions and confidence in me
permeates the pages of this book.
R.B.

To my mom and dad, who, in their own ways,
have modeled the meaning of servant-hood.
N.B.

Contents

Acknowledgments   10
Introduction   11

Section 1:   Before Entering the Pool . . .

1 *Why Go on a Mission Trip?*   15

2 *Orphans and Stain Removers*   21

3 *The Three Stages of Missions Involvement*   27

Section 2:   Toes in the Water

4 *Opening the Investigation*   35

5 *Twenty Ways to Whet Your Group's
Appetite for Service*   39

6 *Preparing Your Students for Ministry*   49

Section 3:   Taking the Plunge

7 *Catching and Sharing the Vision*   61

8 *Drafting a Game Plan*   65

9 *Selecting a Ministry Site*   81

10 *Nuts and Bolts*   93

11 *Now Accepting Applications*   107

12 *On Site*   119

13 *Homeward Bound*   127

Section 4:   Back at the Neighborhood Pool

14 *Serving in Your Own Backyard*   133

15 *Sidewalk Sunday School:*
A Home-Grown Missions Model   137

Section 5:   Resources for World Service

APPENDIX A *Bibliography and Resource List*   155

APPENDIX B *Raising Money for Missions*   159

APPENDIX C *What to Bring on a Mission Trip*   167

APPENDIX D *An Annotated List of Mission and Service*
Organizations   169

Acknowledgments

I'd like to express my deep appreciation to the following people:

Ron Cline, executive director of HCJB Radio—a leader worth modeling myself after.

Carolyn Koons, executive director of the Institute for Outreach Ministries at Azusa Pacific University—a woman whose dream for an outreach into the Mexicali valley has changed thousands of lives . . . including mine.

Candice Pinkowski, secretary at the Center for Student Missions—my faithful assistant and co-worker.

Tricia Brown—for her untold hours of hard work in typing this manuscript.

The elders at the First Evangelical Free Church of Walnut Creek, California—who said yes to my first mission trip.

Dave Courtney and Sue Austin—the student leaders I worked with on my first mission trip in 1978.

John Diehl—the student who directed Sidewalk Sunday School, even when it meant giving up the track team and his after-school job.

Sue Bolhouse Koby—the girl whose dream for ministry started Sidewalk Sunday School, and the most amazing student I have ever worked with.

Robanne—my wife, who has slept in tents, built houses, and made countless children's crafts for Vacation Bible Schools all over the world.

Introduction

In our nearly thirty years of combined youth ministry experience, we've found that nothing brings kids face-to-face with Jesus like mission and service. There is something about putting the challenge to "offer your bodies as living sacrifices, holy and pleasing to God" (Romans 12:1) into practice that changes lives, pure and simple.

We're pleased to bring this handbook to you. In it, you'll find all you'll need to get your youth group involved in mission and service, even if you're starting from scratch. Although this book is primarily Ridge's, and is written from his first-person perspective and experience, we hope you'll catch the scent in these pages of what the Lord has done in both of our lives through mission and service.

This book is meant to be practical and usable, but it's our prayer that you'll come away with more than just ideas, guidelines, budgets, and timelines. We hope you'll also begin to share our heartfelt excitement about serving God in the field. It's been in the dust, and on the street, that we've experienced the thrill of being part of God's great plan of hope and healing in a unique way.

We trust that he will use this book to bring the same thrill into your life, and into the lives of your kids.

Ridge Burns
Noel Becchetti
June 1990

Section 1

Before Entering the Pool . . .

1

Why Go on a Mission Trip?

I T WAS 1977, WALNUT CREEK, CALIFORNIA—the year-end banquet for my high-school youth group. We'd reached the time in our annual event when the seniors were to present their "wills" to the rest of the group. Each senior would share the one event or experience that had affected them the most during their high-school years.

As those twenty-two seniors began to reveal their life-changing experiences, I sat stunned. They didn't mention camp, Sunday school, or their small-group Bible studies. No one pointed to a pivotal talk I'd given, or even times of counseling that I'd spent with them.

Kid after kid said that the Mexicali mission trip was what had changed his or her life. Being involved in practical ministry and helping the poor and oppressed had impacted them in a way unique to their youth group experience.

Maybe it was because for the first time, these kids were able to experience and exercise their faith instead of just talking about it. Or maybe the primitive conditions in which the kids lived during the trip forced them out of their shells and into real Christian fellowship for the first time.

All I know is that when I evaluate my more than fifteen years in youth ministry, the one type of experience that has had the most impact on kids in my youth groups has been mission trips. And these same mission trips have had an unbelievable impact on my life.

Why I Go On Mission Trips

I go on mission trips to see Jesus. One afternoon, I was walking through a refugee camp in Thailand when I saw in the distance a small wooden cross that had been erected over one hut. Curious, I made my way over to that hut. The man of the house, who had no legs, motioned for me to come in. To my surprise, he knew English. As we talked, a horrifying story unfolded.

He had been the president of the national bank of Cambodia and a pastor of one of the local Christian churches. When the Khmer Rouge revolutionaries seized the country, they decided to make him a target of special persecution. They cut off his legs in front of his family, abused his wife, and murdered one of his children. Then they left him on the streets to die. His surviving family somehow nursed him through the journey to the refugee camp.

This man shared his story without anger, bitterness, or malice toward those who had tortured him and his family. He talked about his dependence on Jesus, and how Jesus had helped him through his time of distress. I looked in this man's eyes—and saw the face of Jesus.

I don't see that in the States. I get mad at God when I'm late and get stopped at a traffic light, or consider him unjust when I'm cut off from a parking place that I think is rightfully mine. I lose Jesus in our materialistic society and the busyness of my ministry. I lose that simple dependence on Jesus and simple trust in what God is doing in his world. In order to regain that glimpse of Jesus as he really is, I have to get out from under my umbrella of protection. In that broken-down hut in Thailand, I got to see Jesus.

I go on mission trips to learn about servant-hood. I see practical, everyday models of what it means to live out my life in servant-hood. I meet people like E. G. Von Trutzschler ("Pastor Von" to his many friends), who faithfully ministers week after week in the slums of Tijuana. I meet people like Mary Valencia, a successful businesswoman whom God called to missionary life. She left her home in Santa Fe, New Mexico, and moved to a little island off the coast of Honduras, where she lives on $25 a month. With money she draws from her pension and from individual donors, she runs a small yet effective feeding program for mal-nourished children.

I need to meet people like Pastor Von and Mary Valencia. I need to be confronted with the fact that much of what I call youth ministry is simply entertainment. Seeing firsthand the dependence on God and the commitment to his purposes radiating from these dedicated servants forces me to take a hard look at my commitment to the claims and promises of Jesus Christ.

I go on mission trips to evaluate my own culture. A youth pastor recently told me of the reaction one of his kids had when arriving home from an Easter-week outreach in Tijuana. They had ministered alongside people who were in love with Jesus even though they had so little that they lived off the scraps from the dump. And these same impoverished people were unbelievably generous. They were eager to share what little they had with these kids from an affluent suburb of Portland, Oregon.

One girl in the group was particularly affected by the contrast in values between the Mexican culture and her own. When the vanloads of kids arrived back at the church in Portland, her father came to pick her up in his Mercedes-Benz. As he pulled up in the luxury sedan, the collision of the different cultures hit her, and she threw up.

When I face my own obsession with prosperity and material goods after returning from the Third World or a Los Angeles ghetto, where I see the implorable conditions people live in with great joy, it makes me want to throw up. It makes me take a hard look at my culture, and what God has to say to a church drowning in materialism.

I go on mission trips to experience true Christian fellowship. I was preparing to take a large group of students from Chicago to Ensenada, Mexico, for a two-week summer mission experience. About three months prior to the trip, I took Meg and J.T., two student leaders, with me on the pretrip site inspection.

The trip started like any typical time with students. We were goofing around and talking about soccer, proms, and dating. But when we entered Mexico and saw the poverty of Ensenada, visited orphanages and prisons, and surveyed the Guadalupe Valley where their friends would be ministering in just a few months, something happened to our fellowship.

We began to talk about the very fabric of our lives. We shared things that we would never have been able to talk about back home—our fears, our inadequacies, our temptations, what we hoped God would do in us.

It is within the context of preparing for a life-changing ministry that these kinds of incredible conversations take place. True Christian fellowship is a natural by-product of mission and service.

I go on mission trips to have my heart broken. It was in a small church in the Mexicali valley settlement of Michoacan one Easter week that I gave my heart, in terms of full-time Christian service, to God. My youth group was in charge of the ministry; I was sitting back and watching. Then a little Mexican girl, Anna, came up and asked me to help her with her craft. Then she asked me to help her sing "Jesus Loves Me" in Spanish. It was the beginning of a special relationship that grew during the week.

When it came time to say good-bye, I watched Anna fade out of sight in the rearview mirror of the van, tears streaming down my face. Thinking about the life little Anna faced in her dirt-floor home without running water or sanitation ate at me. God had broken my heart.

God says, "Blessed are those who mourn, for they shall be comforted" (Matthew 5:4). And he has been comforting, and faithful. Over the years, Anna has grown into a fine Christian woman, and, as of this writing, attends Moody Bible Institute on full scholarship.

Every year I go back to that church where I met Anna and where God first broke my heart. I renew the vow I made in that little church and ask God to keep the things that break his heart in the forefront of my heart as well.

True Confessions

It's time to come clean. I've taken hundreds of kids on mission trips. But I don't do it primarily for the kids. Young people are profoundly affected by their experiences on these trips, and I praise God for that. But that's a by-product of my primary reason for leading those groups into service opportunities: what those mission trips and service experiences do to me.

2

Orphans and Stain Removers

JAMES 1:27 SAYS, "Religion that God our Father accepts as pure and faultless is this: to look after orphans and widows in their distress and to keep oneself from being polluted by the world." Sounds simple, right? If we want to be about our Father's business in a way that he will accept, we should go ahead and get cracking. But who are the orphans and widows of today? Does James mean this literally, or is it possible that there are a number of people who are, in various ways, orphans and widows? And if James's words are a mandate to the church, then what are we to do?

The Twenty-first-century Orphans and Widows Society

It's my belief that there at least five kinds of modern-day orphans and widows. And if we're to make a serious commitment to mission and service, we must identify these groups and address their specific needs.

The first of the modern-day orphans and widows are **economic**—people who live below the poverty line. In a five-square-mile area of Los Angeles, nearly 70 percent of the population lives below the poverty line. They cannot afford adequate shelter, food, clothing, or health care.

The second group of today's orphans and widows are **political**—people who have been forced out of their native countries because of revolution, political oppression, or other factors. These include countries like Nicaragua, El Salvador, Cambodia, and Vietnam. Many of these people have fled to the United States, giving us a large pool of national orphans in our own backyards. For example, Los Angeles is now the second largest Salvadoran city in the world. It's also the second largest Nicaraguan city in the world.

Third among the groups of modern-day orphans and widows are **physical**—kids who are detached from their natural moms and dads, not by choice, but by circumstances. These include children from broken homes, latchkey children whose parents have to choose between putting food on the table or being home with their children, kids whose parents have flat-out abandoned them, and underage national orphans who fled their native countries after being separated from their parents, who often were then imprisoned or killed. MacArthur Park in Los Angeles is home for dozens of teenage boys, refugees from war-torn Central America, who have been reduced to male prostitution to earn enough money to survive.

The fourth group of modern day orphans and widows are **elderly**—men and women whose families have left them deserted in rest homes and convalescent hospitals. I know of an inner-city convalescent hospital in Los Angeles that has 133 patients. In November, 1989, there was a total of one visitor to that convalescent home.

The final group of contemporary orphans and widows are **relational**—people who, for whatever reason, are no longer able to relate to people in normal ways. These people are the homeless, the drug dependent, the prostitutes, the street people we stare at when we drive through the wrong part of town.

I was talking not long ago to a prostitute in Los Angeles. I asked her what she would change about her life if she could. She replied, "I want one friend, just one friend, that would treat me as a person, instead of trying to get something from me."

Ring Around the Ministry Collar

It's easy to see that there is plenty for us to do to express our pure and undefiled religion. There is no way that we can earn or work our way to heaven, but once we have accepted Jesus Christ as Lord our responsibility is to those who are disconnected.

The second part of James 1:27 focuses on keeping ourselves unstained by the world. Apparently James links our cleanliness before God and our ability to serve. What are some of the stains that keep us from being effective for God? What particular stain-removing tasks face us as we prepare to step out for God in missions and service? There are three stains, particularly true for us Americans, that directly affect our ability to be used by God in missions and service ministry.

The stain of assumption. Before we take our kids to minister in another culture—particularly one that is materially impoverished—we must face the fact that we are stained by the assumption that because we are Americans, we have the answers for any situation. We also assume that the people we're going to minister to "need" us. Actually, we need these people far more than the other way around.

Recently I called a friend who has a lot of ministry contacts in Los Angeles. He began telling me about an elderly Korean woman who, twice a week at seven o'clock, feeds over 250 homeless men, women, and children out of the back of her Ford Pinto. She had been doing this, week in and week out, for two years. My first response was, "We could really give her a lot of help." His response jarred me: "No, she can really help you." I'd assumed that our kids could help this "poor" lady who for two years has been doing more than the rest of us put together.

The stain of presumption. When we arrive to do ministry, it's easy for us to simplify the problems we see and brainstorm "quick fix" solutions. We observe people in skid row and ask ourselves, "Why don't they all get jobs so they could pay for housing and get food?" If we took the time to get to know the people on skid row, we'd learn some surprising answers to our question. We'd learn that some of them don't have basic job skills. We'd learn that many of them are mentally impaired and have been cast onto the street because of the closure of social service agencies and public hospitals. We'd also learn that many of the men, women, and children of skid row are so insecure about their value in society that they're caught in a sinkhole of discouragement.

Americans by nature are presumptuous. We know what's best for people. We're ready to save the world, preferably within a week or so. Our tendency toward presumption feeds a subtle sense of our own superiority. If these poor people were as smart, as motivated, and as virtuous as we are, we think, they wouldn't be in such a fix.

The stain of materialism. One year our youth group traveled to do a Vacation Bible School at a church in Barranquilla, Columbia. This church was located in a very poor section of town, infested with drugs, poverty, prostitution, and discouragement. Although the church was very poor, it was respected throughout the community for the love and care it demonstrated to the people in the neighborhood.

We were ready to do the greatest VBS ever. We brought in projectors, colored construction paper, crayons, and paints for the kids to play with. We brought brand-new balls and recreation equipment. It was a great week. Hundreds of neighborhood kids flocked to this little church. Kids came to know the Lord.

At the end of the week, the whole church came to the airport to see us off. I felt great about what had happened that week—until the pastor asked me if I could step around the corner for a moment. I was expecting him to shower me with thanks for all that we'd done. Instead, he looked at me with tears in his eyes and said, "Sometimes when groups like yours come, you make me feel so poor." Our fancy balls, modern equipment, and brand-new supplies made the newspaper and charcoal that his kids used the other fifty-one weeks of the year seem so inadequate. Yet he's the pastor of a live and effective church, growing in its faith and meeting needs. Our automatic reliance on our material abundance, although done with good intention, was a crushing discouragement to this faithful, hard-working man of God.

Spiritual Stain Removers

How can we begin the process of spiritual stain removal? First, we can provide our students with practical training prior to their missions trip. In chapter four, I've provided a three-session preparation course that can help your kids confront the issue of spiritual stains.

Second, we can make sure that our students are participating in a missions project that has an element of risk and the potential for failure. These elements provide the challenge that keeps students from becoming overconfident, which often leads to a sense of paternalism. Placing ourselves in risky, even frightening, situations can help make us better listeners and better students.

Third, we need to teach our kids to listen—to observe, to ask questions, and to refrain from jumping to hasty conclusions. At various points in this book, we've provided questionnaires and teaching materials designed to help your students learn the listening process.

Finally, and most important, we can go before the Lord continually, asking him to keep our hearts broken with the things that break his heart. For it's out of a broken heart, one not dirty with the stains of assumption, presumption, or materialism, that we can be the hands and feet of Jesus. 🌴

3

The Three Stages of Missions Involvement

ONE OF THE MAJOR AREAS up for approval at our church's annual budget meeting was the youth mission fund. The members were getting ready to vote on this section of the budget when an older woman, a faithful member of the church for many years, raised her hand to speak. The room grew quiet as she rose and went to the microphone. She paused, looked over at me, and said, "Why are we spending all this money to send kids all around the world when there's so much to do right here in our own community? Why don't our kids get involved in mission and service right here in our own town?"

I began to explain (a little defensively) the reasons why it was important for kids to be involved in overseas missions. But deep down in my soul, I knew she was right. We were spending a lot of money sending kids all over the world and doing very little in our own community. The problem was, how could I get my kids involved in local ministry? When I'd tried, the group had responded with thundering apathy.

There was the time (I pointed out to her) when an older gentleman suggested that our group pay a weekly visit to a local rest home. This sounded like a great idea. I announced it to the kids and set a date for our first visit. The ten of us who went the first week had a great time. We visited the people, ate supper with them, sang with them, and prayed with them. The kids seemed charged up about the ministry.

But the next week, instead of ten we had eight. We still had a good experience, but I noticed that the enthusiasm was wearing down. By the fourth week, it was me and one kid. I found myself resenting the commitment I had made. I was almost mad at the old people for being at their own rest home so I would have to minister to them. We dropped the rest home ministry soon after.

Investigation, Immersion, and Integration

Nonetheless, the question that woman posed at the budget meeting triggered for me a process of learning how to help my kids minister in their own backyards.

In that process, I discovered that I had to have an intentional plan designed to build into kids' lives a hunger for service that would be ultimately satisfied only by serving in their own community. I needed to develop stages of involvement that culminated with a homegrown and home-centered service ministry. Through trial and error, I learned that there are three stages of mission involvement that lead to a lifestyle of service: investigation, immersion, and integration.

Investigation gives kids a taste of missions, helping them gain a basic understanding of what service ministry is all about. In the investigation stage, we provide opportunities for our kids to get their feet wet—maybe for a day, maybe just for a couple of hours—with creative, low-cost activites. (Chapter five outlines twenty such feet-wetting exercises.)

Immersion allows kids to actually be part of the solution to the world's problems in Jesus' name. They plan, direct, and implement their own response to the Great Commission in the form of a mission trip. It might be a weekend, a week, two weeks, or a whole summer. But whatever length and whatever location, one factor is essential: This trip is out of the kids' local environment.

Although it may seem backward to send kids far away so that they can serve up close, I've learned that it's essential to give kids their first missions experience away from home, where everything they encounter is unfamiliar—the people they meet, the place they sleep, the food they eat, the languages they hear. In such a new and often unsettling environment, kids are much more open to God's call on their lives, both in the field and at home. And exploring a new environment appeals to kids' sense of adventure—an important component of any mission trip that I'll discuss further in chapter four.

As kids' hunger for service builds through investigation and immersion, the seed of *integration* will begin to grow. Sooner or later, one of our kids will ask why the group should wait until the next mission trip to be involved in service. They'll be ready and willing to explore opportunities to serve in their local communities. Without bringing our kids to this point, we haven't really fulfilled the Great Commission.

Checking our Personal Missions Pulse

But before we can begin to involve our kids in the stages of mission involvement, we need to check our personal missions pulse in three key areas.

Do we believe that kids can make a difference? Odd as it may seem, there are many youth workers who don't. We believe that kids are the church of tomorrow, therefore they need to wait until tomorrow before they really serve.

Recently I met a man on the streets of Los Angeles who shared an amazing testimony. Tony served in the medical corps in Vietnam as a doctor. When he returned home from the war, the hostility he experienced as a returning Vietnam veteran so devastated him that he dropped out of society to live on the streets of Los Angeles. Bitter, broken, and abusing alcohol and drugs, Tony was not a happy man.

Two years ago, he was standing by a fire barrel when a church van pulled up. A group of kids got out of the van and started handing out tuna fish sandwiches. He was somehow touched by the shy, awkward high-school girl who gave him his sandwich.

He began asking her questions, trying to find out why she'd come down to skid row to feed someone like him. Although the poor girl was terrified, she shared with Tony what God had done in her life. Tony then asked this girl how he could get to know God. She was totally unprepared to share her faith, but she had a copy of the *Four Spiritual Laws* in her pocket. Pulling it out, she awkwardly plowed through the booklet with Tony. When she asked Tony if he would like to receive Jesus Christ and accept him as his personal savior, Tony told me, "Something happened to me, and I really sensed that's what I should do." This high-school girl led Tony to Jesus Christ.

Tony continues to live on the street—only now as a medical minister for Jesus Christ. He is the only doctor on skid row who makes house calls. Why? Because one high-school girl made a difference.

Do we have a heart for missions? John Perkins says, "Before you do, you gotta be." Before we can do missions, we've got to experience it for ourselves, to have our hearts broken with the things that break the heart of God.

What can we do to develop our own heart for missions? We can read some of the biographies of the great missionaries of the Christian church. Our spiritual boundaries will explode when we read the amazing stories of these faithful servants of God. Several of these books are listed in the Bibliography (Appendix A). I personally recommend Robert Lupton's book, *Theirs is the Kingdom* (Harper and Row, 1989). It's a powerful testimony from a modern-day missionary.

We can also get our own feet wet in local mission and service—working in a soup kitchen, visiting young prisoners in the local juvenile detention center, helping out at the rescue mission. And we can serve as hosts for missionaries who visit our churches. As we get acquainted with these outstanding men and women of God, we hear straight from the source the amazing ways God is moving all over the world.

If cross-cultural ministry is new to us, we may find ourselves feeling uncomfortable, awkward, and inadequate as we take our first steps into the feet-wetting process. That's okay! It's normal. And service ministry *will* bring out our real inadequacies. Mission work brings us face-to-face with our own utter dependency on God's power and grace like no other ministry I know. And entering into the struggle with our own inadequacies will make us sensitive to our kids' anxieties when they begin the same process.

Do we understand that mission and service requires a substantial investment of money and time? There are no shortcuts in the commitments required to take kids on a mission trip. It requires raising money, raising consciousness, and raising many questions that we'd rather not deal with—questions like, "Why are we taking kids on mission trips? We used to go to summer camp—and summer camp is cheaper and safer."

That statement is true—summer camp *is* cheaper and safer. But is a steady diet of cheap, safe religious activities the methodology God intends to use to raise up a new generation of servants who will hunger for a lifestyle of service?

Reaping the Harvest

Paul's admonition that we reap what we sow (Galatians 6:7–10) is nowhere truer than in the area of service. If we spoon-feed our kids, and ourselves, on a pablum diet of safe, familiar youth ministry, we'll reap a harvest of timid spectators with delicate spiritual digestive systems. But as we challenge our kids to step out and put themselves on the line for God in Christian service, we'll stand amazed as we watch the harvest of vibrant, growing Christian young men and women come in from the field. It's more than worth the investment.

Ready to begin sowing the seeds? Let's start by exploring how we can help our kids to get their mission toes in the water.

Toes in the Water

4

Opening the Investigation

I HAD JUST FINISHED A TALK on student missions at a high-school camp in the mountains of Southern California. As I stood by the podium fielding the usual post-talk questions, I noticed one guy lingering near the back of the group, a troubled look on his face. He looked too old to be a high-schooler, so I figured he must be a youth pastor. *I wonder what he wants to ask?* I thought. *Maybe he was upset with something I said.*

I was right—and wrong. He was a youth pastor. But when he came up to me after the last student had departed for lunch, I discovered that he wasn't upset with my talk; it was his youth group that was troubling him. "Ridge," he began, "I agree with everything you're saying about the importance of mission and service. But how can I get my kids off square one? Every time I try to introduce the subject of missions, my kids shrink back. It's like they're afraid of the idea. Is my group strange?"

We spent some time discussing the situation, and I assured him that he was not alone. It sounds surprising when we consider the growing number of young people becoming involved in mission and service, but there are many kids who are afraid of the idea of a mission trip. These fears are normal, and we need to be aware of them as we try to get our kids started in the first stage of mission involvement—helping them to open the investigation.

Frankly, I'm Scared

First, kids *fear the unknown*. A mission trip is a step into the unknown for most kids, and that frightens them. Kids today are cautious about making commitments. Given the unstable world they find themselves in, it's understandable. The insecurity that kids see all around—broken families, cloudy economic futures, major political upheavals that seem to happen overnight—pushes them toward the comfort of the known.

Second, kids today are so used to being spectators, not participants, that to challenge them to be involved in a mission program brings them face-to-face with their *fear of involvement*. It would be nice to say that youth ministry has helped kids to become more action-oriented, but too often that is not the case. Our kids are more accustomed to being entertained about their faith than being challenged in their faith.

Third, challenging kids to step out in service to the Lord brings to the surface their *fear of their own spiritual weakness*. Ministry that challenges kids to share their faith and publicly demonstrate their walk with God is threatening, and their own spiritual weakness may cause them to shrink back. This, I believe, is a positive. Our kids—and all of us—*need* to be shaken from our spiritual complacency. Mission trips and service projects force us to face our own weaknesses and develop a fresh dependence on the love and power of God.

The final fear that holds kids back from missions isn't theirs—it's *their parents' fears about their involvement*. These fears are two-pronged. First, parents naturally worry for their children's safety, and any mission trip contains a certain element of risk. The second fear is more subtle, and dangerous. When kids come off a mission trip, they begin to ask questions about their culture, their lives, and their faith that some parents don't want to hear. It's unnerving for parents to hear their own children challenging them about their commitment to Jesus. It's particularly unnerving when their children are right.

Lighting the Spark

So, to repeat the question put to me by the troubled youth worker, how can we get our kids, particularly those young people who are fearful of the idea of mission and service, off of square one? How can we help them to begin the investigation process? There are three immediate steps we can take:

Understand and utilize the role of adventure in mission trips. For most of our kids, up to 75 percent of their motivation for going on their first mission trip will be adventure—the travel, the new experiences, the chance to see and do things they've never done before. No more than 25 percent of their motivation will be response to God's call. These are arbitrary percentages, but in my experience, they usually hold true.

Take, for example, my rest home fiasco. That ministry failed because I tried to get kids involved in a long-term, local commitment before I had developed in them a hunger for mission and service. The nurturing of an appetite for mission and service starts with short, exciting mission experiences that allow kids to begin to sense that they need to be involved in a greater way.

It's because of this adventure element that mission trips can take so much flak from cost-conscious parents and church boards. And we may hinder more than help our cause when we focus more on our destination than on our ministry objectives. But if this is part of the reality of getting kids involved in mission and service, we need to accept it for what it is and use it properly.

It's during those first missions experiences that kids move from a focus on adventure to a focus on who God is and his call on their lives. But if kids are to have this encounter with God, we've first got to get them to go on the trip—and understand their motivations for doing so.

Move with the movers. Rather than wait for the whole group to catch the vision, move ahead with the kids who are interested in getting involved in missions. Don't worry if it's only three or four kids; go ahead and start with them.

My first mission experience involved myself and three of my kids handing out clothes and food at a street mission in downtown Oakland, California. But that day with those three kids planted the seeds for great things later on with the whole youth group.

Start small. We believe success only comes in large numbers. Yet sometimes we need to start small. It's tough to get a large group of kids excited about something new. When that new something is frightening, like mission and service, it's even tougher. But when we start small and move with the movers, we begin to build a core of excitement and leadership within our group. When those three kids who handed out food and clothes in downtown Oakland shared the joy and excitement of their experience with the rest of the group, the spark of interest of the whole group toward mission and service began to sizzle. Our first trip to Mexicali wasn't far off.

First Steps

When we understand the role of adventure in missions, give ourselves the freedom to move with the few interested kids, and commit to starting small, we begin to see the dozens of "feet-wetting" mission experiences available all around us. We don't have to plan a trip to Mexico to give our kids that first taste of a new adventure; there are plenty of creative ways to continue the investigation, as we'll see in the next chapter. 🌴

5

Twenty Ways to Whet Your Group's Appetite for Service

A GREAT WAY TO CONTINUE the investigation process with our kids is to whet their appetite with real-life experiences and mini-adventures that can be done inexpensively, locally, and in short periods of time. The following list, though not exhaustive, outlines twenty specific ways to expose young people to mission and service "up close and personal."

Ride a Public Bus

Plan a youth activity that requires your kids to ride a public bus. In a typical urban center, such as Los Angeles, public transit is the only means of transportation for up to 50 percent of the population. Arm your kids with questions to ponder while they're riding the bus: What do the other people on the bus dress like? Where do you think they are going? What is the average age of a person riding a public bus?

Discuss your kids' observations together when they gather after their bus ride—perhaps at a major city park.

Visit an Inner-City Church

Take your kids to a Sunday service in an inner-city church. These churches range from small storefront congregations to large sanctuaries that hold thousands of people. Your kids will have the opportunity to rub shoulders with Christians from a different culture and experience a church service that will be quite unlike what they're normally used to. Discuss the similarities and differences between the congregations and the services with your kids on the ride home.

Take a Tour of the Inner City

Instead of taking the freeway around a major city on your next trip, take the kids through the inner city. Take them through the homeless section—there is one in every major urban center. Just seeing the people and the poverty is enough to give kids a hunger to be part of the solution. Your ride may prove to have more impact than the event you're going to!

Sleep in a Box

Take a supply of cardboard boxes with you on your next summer camp or retreat. At some point during the event, have your kids spend one night sleeping in a box, with nothing but their clothes and perhaps an old blanket for warmth.

The next morning, have your group discuss what it felt like to be, for one night, among the thousands of people living in boxes in America. Have them reflect on one or more of the verses listed in the Bible study found in chapter six.

Sunday School in the Cold

One Sunday morning, instead of having Sunday school in your warm building, bring some blankets and old coats from a thrift shop and have your kids meet outside in the cold. Discuss the value of shelter, and the blessing of having a warm place to meet.

Have a Lockout

Instead of locking the kids in the church overnight, lock them out of the church. Restrict them to a controlled area on the church grounds. Have boxes for them to sleep in, fire barrels or barbecues for them to stay warm around, and one (only one) chemical toilet on the grounds for their use. Do not provide running water.

Arrange for some people in your church to drive up and feed them a meal out of the back of their car. After their meal, let them experience a night out in the cold. You can plan a Bible study by flashlight related to God's concern for the poor.

Have your kids discuss their experience the next morning before they depart for home.

Shantytown Scavenger Hunt

Give your students thirty minutes to walk out into the surrounding neighborhood and find things they could build a shelter with—a box, newspapers, an old tent they find in an alley or behind a store. They can go up to people's doors and ask for things that they could live with. The goal is to find enough items to build a Shantytown for the evening.

When they arrive with their scavenged materials, give them an additional thirty minutes to build a Shantytown in the parking lot of the church. If you can find a fifty-five-gallon drum, or even part of a barbecue, you can build a fire in the barbecue to increase the shantytown feel.

After they've set up their shantytown or exhausted their thirty minutes, gather them around the fire and ask the following questions:

- How did it feel to have to scavenge?
- How did it feel to have to beg?
- What would it be like if you had to live like this night after night?

Play Calendar Pay-off

Print a calendar that has a space for each day of the month. In each space, enter an instruction that will determine how much money each teen must give that day. The instruction should be humorous, and should vary the amount from one day to the next.

When the month is up, the kids bring in the money they owe. Give the money to a local mission project.

A variation of this would be to print the instruction for each day on separate sheets of paper, fold them, and staple them so they are concealed until the end of the day. The instruction can then be a "fine" for certain things done or not done. For example, it might say "Pay five cents for each class that you were late to today," or "Pay twenty-five cents if you forgot to brush your teeth." (See sample chart on following page.)

Allow a space on the calendar where kids can write how much they owe each day. They can just total it up at the end of the month. You might add one "extra" space for them to give any amount they choose. This approach adds a little fun and variety to giving.

Calendar Pay-off

1. One cent for each pair of shoes and sneakers you own.
2. Three cents if you disobeyed your parents today.
3. Five cents if you forgot to use a deodorant today.
4. Four cents if you have *blue* eyes.
5. Ten cents if you did not clean and straighten up your room.
6. Fifteen cents if you did not attend *church* today.
7. Five cents if you washed your hair today.
8. One cent for each time you talked on the telephone today.
9. Five cents if you get up before seven a.m.
10. Three cents if you wore any type of jeans today.
11. One cent for each soda you drank today.
12. Two cents for each hour of sleep you had last night.
13. One cent for each mile you live away from your church.
14. Two cents if you have a hole in your socks.
15. Five cents if you did not do your homework.
16. Two cents if you have your license to drive a car.
17. Four cents if you have *brown* eyes.
18. One cent for each letter in your last name.
19. Ten cents if you shaved anything today!
20. Five cents if you wore blue today.
21. Five cents for each test you had today.
22. One cent for each class you had today.
23. Fifty cents if you were not at teen choir tonight.
24. Ten cents if you did not eat breakfast at home this morning.
25. Three cents for each time you failed to make your bed this week.
26. Twenty cents if you did not donate any money yesterday.
27. Ten cents if you have a pair of Nikes.
28. Three cents for each pair of gloves you own.
29. Three cents if you didn't read your Bible today.
30. Ten cents because it is almost the last day to pay.
31. Fifteen cents if you wore the color red today.

Work in a Soup Kitchen

Find a local agency that feeds the homeless and sign your kids up to prepare and serve a meal. The physical contact with those who are so broken is a powerful experience.

A Water Walk

One of the big problems in the Third World is getting safe drinking water. Most students don't realize that easy access to safe water is a real gift. Have each of your kids come to the church with a bucket, empty plastic bottle, or similar container. Take them to a stream or other water source far enough away from your church to make it a considerable walk. Their assignment is to carry enough water back to the church to fill a fifty-five-gallon drum. When they are finished, point out that fifty-five gallons of water is enough to keep a family of four alive for three weeks in Kenya.

Discuss what it means for us to have safe water available at our fingertips.

Spend Time in Junk Cars

After obtaining permission, take your kids to an auto wrecking yard and have them spend thirty minutes in a junk car. Give each student the list of questions below to think about as they sit in the car:

- Can you imagine this being your home? What would you do to make it better?
- What would be the hardest part about living here?
- Circle the kinds of people you think would live in a junk car:

lazy	families	drug addicts
poor	sick	uneducated
women	drunks	non-Americans

- What do you think Jesus would do if he came upon people living in junk cars?
- Read Matthew 25:35-36: "For I was hungry and you gave me something to eat, I was thirsty and you gave me something to drink, I was a stranger and you invited me in, I needed clothes and you clothed me, I was sick and you looked after me, I was in prison and you came to visit me." How might that passage apply in this situation?

Deliver Meals on Wheels

Most major cities have a program called "Meals on Wheels." This provides hot meals for the elderly or people who cannot produce meals on their own. Have your group (supervised by a responsible adult) deliver Meals on Wheels for a day. Your kids will be able to go into the homes and apartments and rooms of some of the poorest people in your community and give them a meal in Jesus' name.

Visit a VA or a County Hospital

Have your kids spend an hour in the waiting room of a VA or County Hospital. After you return to the church, have your group discuss these questions:
- How does the kind of medical care I saw differ from the kind that my family would give me?
- How would I feel if that were the only hospital I could go to?

Cook a $5 Meal

Divide your youth group into teams of five. Take them to the grocery store and give $5 to each team. Instruct each group that the $5 is all the money they'll have to purchase food for the next twenty-four hours. After they've purchased the food, bring them back to the church. Have a pot and an open fire or a simple hot plate for each team. Instruct them to prepare their food and eat their meal together. After they've finished and cleaned up their dishes, lead the group in prayer for those in their community who are living on a dollar's worth of food a day.

Video Interviews

Take a video camera and one of your student leaders out into the community and interview some of the poor and disenfranchised people. Talk to a prostitute, a homeless person, an elderly person, and others you might find. Ask them questions you think your students might ask. Then one night at youth meeting, show the video to the rest of your kids and let them see firsthand the poverty and oppression in their own hometown.

Rich-Poor Questionnaire

Using the questionnaire below, survey people in a suburban mall. Then take the same questionnaire and go to a shopping district in the poorer section of town. When you've gathered the results, compare the answers and talk about the differences in outlook between the rich and the poor.
1. What is the biggest problem facing the city right now?
2. If you were mayor for one day, what is the one thing you would do?
3. Who is Jesus?

Simulation Games

There are a variety of games that you can play with your students that allow them to experience the inequities of the world and the problems of the homeless. Two of the more effective simulation games I've used are:
- Bafa Bafa—a cross-cultural simulation experience. It can be ob-

tained through Simili II, P.O. Box 910, Del Mar, CA 92014 (619) 755-0272.

- The Luna Game—a humorous game that provides a lesson in cross-cultural communication. It can be obtained through World Christian, P.O. Box 40010, Pasadena, CA 91104.

A more extensive selection of games is available in the *Handbook of Simulation Games in Social Education* by Ron Stadskleu (Institute of High Research, University of Alabama Press).

Volunteer at a Rescue Mission

Rescue missions are in constant need of volunteers. They are always looking for youth groups to cook, clean, sort clothes, and perform a variety of other tasks. This kind of experience both helps the mission and puts your kids in direct contact with the homeless population.

Guest Speakers

Bring a homeless person from a local rescue mission in as a guest speaker for your youth group. Have a time for questions and answers—about what it's like to live on the street, what that person's hopes and dreams are, what he or she fears.

Prayer Tour of the Inner City

Assemble your kids in a church van and drive around the inner city, pausing in front of spots you've preselected for your kids to lead out in public prayer while they're in the van. For example, you could stop in front of
- An abortion clinic.
- A skid row hotel.
- A group of prostitutes on the corner.

- A soup kitchen for the homeless.
- A rescue mission.
- The county hospital.
- The police station.

6

Preparing Your Students for Ministry

PART OF THE BASIC PREPARATION for mission and service involves intentional preparation. There are a number of helpful resources available to prepare kids for mission and service, many of which are mentioned in the Bibliography (Appendix A).

In addition, I've provided the following three preparation sessions. They range from 60 to 110 minutes each and are designed to prepare your kids in three key areas: team unity, healthy attitudes, and proper motivation. You can use them as they are, or modify them to suit your specific needs.

Session One: One for All and All for One

Goals for Session One

Establish team unity and cohesiveness; develop appropriate team expectations.

Supplies Needed for Session One

Legos   Balloons
Marker pens   Butcher or construction paper

Session One Meeting Plan*

Introductions—ten minutes

Have all team members and adults who are going on the trip introduce themselves. Each person's introduction should include the following items:

1. Name.
2. The name of the city and the hospital where he or she was born.
3. The date he or she became a Christian.

Lego Get-Acquainted Game—fifteen minutes

Divide your group into three teams. Each team is given one of the identical piles of Legos. The object of the game is to be the first team to duplicate the object that the leader has made before the session started.

The trick is that the model is placed in another room. Each team sends one representative there who can study the object for just ten seconds. That person then goes back to his or her team and begins to describe how to properly put the pile of Legos together. Every thirty seconds another person from each team can go and observe the project for ten more seconds.

* Note: Before Session One begins, divide the Legos into four piles. Each pile should have identical amounts of Legos by color, shape, and size. Take one of those identical piles and make a fairly complex object out of it. That object will be the model for the rest of the teams to imitate.

As the game develops, there will be more and more confusion and conflict in terms of whose descriptions are correct and whose are not. This process yields valuable insight as to each team's natural leaders, natural followers, nonparticipants, and how well each team can work together.

If no team has won after fifteen minutes, end the game. Bring your group back together and ask some questions:

- What did you find out about each other?
- Who was the leader? Why? How did the rest of the team feel about the leader?
- Did everyone participate? If not, why not?
- What new skills did you discover in your teammates?

Body Balloon Burst—five minutes

Everyone in the room is part of the body. Those whose last names begin with A–G are a foot; H–N, a hand; O–S, a mouth; and T–Z, a rear end.

When the leader calls "GO!" the kids form complete bodies of six people each—two hands, two feet, one mouth, and one rear end. Once a body is complete, the two feet carry one of the hands up to the leader and receive a balloon. Only the hand can carry the balloon. The two hands then hold the balloon while the mouth blows it up. Once the balloon is blown up, the rear end sits on it. The first body to pop its balloon is the winner.

This game graphically illustrates that a body is made up of many parts, each with a different contribution to make. After the game is over, read 1 Corinthians 12:12–26, and briefly discuss how the cooperation (or lack thereof) they experienced in the game relates to Paul's teaching on the body of Christ.

Trip Logistics—ten minutes

Discuss the logistics of your upcoming mission trip. You may want to do some of the following:

1. Pass out a "Things to Bring" list.
2. Pass out permission slips.

3. Present your fund-raising plan.
4. Discuss the payment schedule for kids' fees and set deadlines.
5. Pass out a schedule for all required meetings for the trip.
6. Show slides of the project. If you don't have any, give a complete verbal description of the site and the purpose of the trip.
7. Take time for questions and answers.

Team Covenant—twenty minutes

Get a large piece of butcher or construction paper. You'll need to take this piece of paper with you, so don't use a blackboard or chalkboard. Ask your team the following questions:

- How do we need to treat one another to make this mission experience all that God wants it to be?
- What kinds of attitudes do we need to have toward one another?
- How should we behave toward one another?

Answers could include statements like: "We need to listen to one another." So you might write on the paper, "Listen," or "Be good listeners."

You may want "Pray together" as a behavioral objective. You may want to have a good time in the Lord, and just have a lot of fun together. Write those words on the paper.

Once you've gotten fifteen to twenty different characteristics on the paper, go through them again and ask the kids whether or not they agree on what's been written down. Some of the charactersitics may need to be removed or altered, and new characteristics may be added.

When you've agreed to a list of ten to twelve characteristics, that becomes your covenant. Have all the kids sign the covenant as a symbol of their commitment to carrying out the characterstics listed.

Take the covenant with you on the trip and display it in a prominent place at the site, such as where you eat or sleep, so kids are reminded daily of their training sessions and of the things they agreed to be to each other.

You can also bring the covenant out during your trip—perhaps at an evening campfire or afterglow service—and have the group evaluate how well they think they are doing in meeting the standards of the covenant.

Session Two: Attitude Check

Goals for Session Two

Articulate the attitudes the group will need to have to survive and grow during the mission trip.

Supplies Needed for Session Two

World View Survey
Phone Chain Chart (sample found in chapter eight, page 69)
Trip Guidelines (sample found in chapter eleven, page 112)
Masking Tape

Session Two Meeting Plan

Logistics—ten minutes

Be sure to discuss the following:
1. Fund-raising plan.
2. Pass out the phone chain and discuss it as a communication tool.
3. Pass out the guidelines for the trip.
4. Take time for questions and answers.

Shantytown Scavenger Hunt—forty to sixty minutes

The description for this exercise can be found on page 41 in chapter five.

World View Survey—ten minutes

While still in the Shantytown, pass out pencils and the World View Survey (see following page). After the kids take the survey, give them the answers and talk to them about the complexity of the problems and the importance of being part of the solution.

World View Survey

1. Approximately _____ million people are malnourished worldwide.
   - a. 100   b. 500   c. 750   d. 1,000
2. Malnutrition is the underlying cause in _____ of all deaths of children under five years of age.
   - a. one-quarter   b. one-half   c. one-tenth   d. one-third
3. Americans, who make up 6 percent of the world's population, consume about _____ percent of the world's non-reusable resources.
   - a. 14   b. 27   c. 45   d. 40
4. In the 83 poorest countries, _____ percent of the people control 80 percent of the land.
   - a. 3   b. 13   c. 23   d. 43
5. The world's population is _____ billion.
   - a. 3.5   b. 4   c. 6   d. 4.8
6. _____ percent of the world's population lacks access to safe water and adequate sanitation.
   - a. 20   b. 25   c. 33   d. 50
7. There are approximately _____ hungry people in the United States.
   - a. 100,000   b. 5 million   c. 10 million   d. 20 million
8. The average food stamp benefit per person, per meal works out to _____.
   - a. 17 cents   b. 47 cents   c. $2   d. unlimited
9. Programs for the poor in the United States (such as welfare, food stamps, Medicare, subsidies) account for _____ percent of the federal budget.
   - a. 7.5   b. 10   c. 18   d. 25
10. Last year, _____ percent of the grain needed to feed all the people in the world was produced.
    - a. 30   b. 50   c. 100   d. 200
11. Approximately _____ percent of the world today is nominally Christian.
    - a. 15   b. 30   c. 40   d. 50
12. Today, _____ percent of the world's population has heard the Good News of the Gospel of Jesus Christ.
    - a. 1–3   b. 5–7   c. 20–25   d. 30–33

ANSWERS: 1, d; 2, d; 3, d; 4, a; 5, d; 6, d; 7, d; 8, b; 9, a; 10, d; 11, b; 12, b.

Reflective Reading—ten minutes

Read the following excerpt called "Christmas Again" from Robert Lupton's book *Theirs is the Kingdom* (Harper and Row, 1989, reprinted by permission):

> "Christmas again." The words are barely audible, but his wife knows the feelings. She sees the hurt come into his eyes when the kids come home from school talking about what they want for Christmas. It's the same expression she sees on the faces of other unemployed fathers around the housing project.
>
> She knows this year will be no different than the last. All her husband's hustle, his pick-up jobs, his day labor will not be enough to pay for presents under the tree. They will do well to keep the heat on. His confident, promising discussions will allow the children their dreams a little while longer.
>
> She will cover for him again because she knows that he's a good man. His lies are his wishes. His flawed attempts to let his children know what the older ones know, but will never admit, that the gifts are not from daddy.
>
> He will not go with her to stand in the free toy lines with all the others. He cannot bring himself to do it. It's too stark a reminder of his own impotence. And if their home is blessed again this year with a visit from a Christian family bearing food and beautifully wrapped presents for the kids, he will stay in the bedroom until they're gone.
>
> He will leave the smiling and the graciousness to his wife. His joy for the children will be genuine, but so is the heavy ache in his stomach as his image of himself as the provider is dealt another blow.
>
> Christmas. That wonderful, awful time when giving hearts glow warm and bright, while fading embers of a poor man's pride are doused black.

After reading that, ask your students the following questions:
- How would you feel if you were a father unable to provide gifts for your children at Christmastime?
- How would you feel about the people who came to give you gifts?

- How would you feel if your father was a hard worker, but could not provide enough money to buy Christmas presents?
- What kinds of attitudes might prevent people from feeling so bad about receiving our help?
- What kinds of attitudes might build up the self-image of those we minister to?

Skills Rehearsal—twenty minutes

Devote the rest of your time to practicing skills that you will be using on your mission trip. For example, you may want to practice your Vacation Bible School, do construction preparation, pack supplies, or complete other tasks related to your trip.

Session Three: Search Me and Know Me

Goals for Session Three

Encourage your kids toward the right motivation for the trip—to go in the spirit of the Lord and not in their own flesh.

Supplies Needed for Session Three

Crayons or marker pens
Newsprint or construction paper

Session Three Meeting Plan

Four-Way Picture—thirty minutes

Pass out a piece of paper and a crayon or marker pen to every student. Have each kid divide the piece of paper into four equal quadrants. Give them twenty minutes to draw the following pictures in each quadrant:

In one quadrant, have them draw a picture of the destination of your mission trip—Los Angeles, Appalachia, Nicaragua, Zaire, wherever. This picture can be any size and perspective they want—an overview of the whole city or country or some particular aspect of the area.

In the second quadrant, have them draw a picture that articulates or symbolizes their greatest fear concerning the trip.

In the third quadrant, have them draw a symbol that represents their feelings about the group going on the trip—not stick figures, but a symbol of some kind—such as people holding hands, a group all going in the same direction, a group with one member left standing outside.

In the fourth quadrant, have them draw a picture of God.

After they've completed their pictures, have them go around the circle and share their pictures with each other. When they've finished sharing, have them sign their pictures and instruct them to bring their pictures with them on the trip. From these pictures, you can gain several things: insights into their preconceived perceptions of the ministry site; a picture of their perceived fears; a handle on how the group feels about each other. And the picture of God will help you understand how they feel about the Lord they serve.

As they share their pictures, try to catch the meaning behind each drawing by getting the kids to describe what's there.

Bible Study—twenty to thirty minutes

A. Read Deuteronomy 15:7–11; Psalm 9:9; Isaiah 25:4, 61:1. Then answer the following questions:
1. From these verses, how would you describe God's attitude toward the poor?
2. What do you think our attitude should be toward the people discussed in these verses?
3. Why do you think our attitudes are sometimes different? What causes us to have the wrong attitudes?
B. Read Proverbs 14:21–31, 19:17, 28:27; James 2:12–13; 1 John 3:17–18. Then answer the following questions:
1. How can we express our love for God?
2. How are blessings in our own lives connected to our concern for the poor?

C. Read Deuteronomy 15:7–11; Matthew 5:42, 19:21–22; Luke 11:41; Isaiah 58:7–8, Matthew 25:34–43; Proverbs 29:7; Isaiah 1:17. Then answer the following questions:

1. What three ways has God given us to care for the poor?
2. What can we do to care for the poor?
3. What is our church doing to care for the poor?

Finally, ask these discussion questions:

1. Why are the poor, poor?
2. How would you respond to the statement, "There will always be poor people, and there's nothing you can do about it"?
3. If you were President of the United States, what policies would you initiate to alleviate the problems of the poor in the world?
4. If you were God, how would you want the Christian church in America to respond to the needs of the poor?
5. Write a definition for the word *poor*.

Skills and Logistics Rehearsal—twenty-five minutes

Continue your preparation for the on-site ministry and the logistics of the trip. Concentrate on the skills and tasks you'll specifically need for your trip.

Prayer Together—fifteen minutes

Close this session with prayer together—perhaps even communion. Make this a time when your kids commit themselves to the Lord to do great things in his Spirit. 🌴

Taking the Plunge

Catching and Sharing the Vision

7

ONCE YOUR STUDENTS have developed an appetite for missions through the process of investigation, they'll be ready to be immersed in a more intentional mission opportunity—a weekend, week-long, or longer mission and service trip.

There are two ways to organize this kind of mission experience. One way is to hook up with an organization that provides the kinds of experiences that you're looking for. For example, if you want your kids to build shelters for people who do not have safe and decent housing, Habitat for Humanity has dozens of such projects in the U.S. and around the world. Organizations like World Servants, Youth With A Mission (YWAM), and the Center for Student Missions provide programs that youth groups can plug directly into. With these programs, you sign up your group, pay a fee, complete whatever preparatory materials the organization sends you, and get your kids to the ministry site. The organization provides the logistical and administrative support for your ministry. (A more complete listing of these and other organizations can be found in Appendix D.) These are wonderful ways to get kids involved in mission and service without expending a lot of time. They are particularly helpful for the inexperienced youth worker, but they are usually more expensive than planning and doing the trip yourself.

In this section, I focus on the second alternative—planning, preparing, funding, and running your own mission trip. You'll find everything needed to develop your own mission experience.

Evaluation Time

Before you begin the planning process, take stock of your situation. First, *evaluate your group*. What kinds of ministry opportunities have they responded to in the past? How effective were those opportunities? What definition would they give to the word "missions"?

You also need to *evaluate your church*. What kind of mission program do they have? What kind of support can you expect from them for a youth mission trip? What resistance might you run into? Has the church had experience with youth missions in the past? How recently? Was the experience good or bad? Would your pastor support a youth missions trip? How about the church missions committee? And how do you think the parents of your kids will respond to the idea of a youth missions trip?

Then, *evaluate your funding situation*. How large is the youth budget? Is any of it available for missions? Would you be able to fund part of the trip out of the church's missionary budget? What other resources are available?

Approval, Anyone?

Your next step is to *gain approval for the general idea of a youth missions trip*. The first person you need to consult is your senior pastor. Ask him if he would approve of the general concept of a youth mission trip. Don't worry about bringing up specific dates or locations. That will come later. By bringing your senior pastor into the decision-making process early, you're demonstrating your respect for his authority and encouraging his input. An informed senior pastor is likely to feel more comfortable with your leadership.

After you've talked with your senior pastor, set an appointment to meet with the church missions committee. This can often be one of the most powerful committees in the church, as they usually control a lot of money. They can sometimes be protective of the missionaries they support. Some members may be retired missionaries who had bad experiences with short-term mission teams when they were in the field. When you meet with them, listen to their concerns respectfully and allow them to have early input into the mission trip. They will often provide valuable tips to help you plan the trip, and by gaining their involvement, you can more easily win their approval.

Finally, *ask your students for their approval*. Rather than first putting it up to a vote of the whole group, get with a few of your key students or your leadership council and explain your vision for a youth mission trip. If you've already spent time getting your group into the investigation process, your student leaders will likely be enthusiastic about the idea. As they catch your vision for the mission trip, they'll begin to share that vision throughout the rest of the group.

After your kids have had some time to discuss the idea among themselves, bring the concept of a mission trip to the whole group. You'll likely have a group of excited young people ready to embark on the next elements of the planning process: developing your student leadership team and developing the goals for your trip. 🌴

8

Drafting a Game Plan

ONCE YOUR YOUTH GROUP is on board with the idea of a mission trip, get your key student leaders into place. I've based my planning for student mission trips on the premise that the kids should be in charge. Students should make the decisions and take the responsibility for the project. The organizational chart reproduced on the following page reflects that priority.

Student Director

The Student Director is responsible for managing the logistics of the project. The young person you're looking for will fulfill the following job description.

Student Director
Primary Functions
1. Direct and facilitate the logistical functions of the First Church mission project in an organized manner.

2. Create the environment for missions education to take place during a two-week experience next summer.
3. Ensure that the mission project achieves the goals articulated in the missions statement.

Responsibilities

1. Secure the necessary transportation for the mission project.
2. Work with, encourage, and support the adult leadership who are part of the mission project.
3. Create and execute a Vacation Bible School or camp ministry through a collection of student committees.
4. Supervise the work program.
5. Encourage, disciple, and coordinate plans with the Student Shepherd.
6. Coordinate and facilitate proper food services for the mission project.
7. Develop and coordinate the publicity for the mission project.
8. Attend all mission project leadership meetings.

Organizational Chart

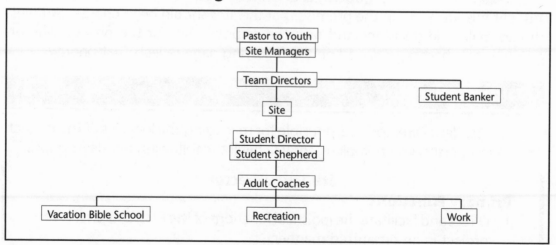

9. Coordinate plans with and encourage the Site Manager.

Supervision Received
Youth Pastor

Supervision Exercised
Mission Project Team

Qualifications
A high-school junior or senior who has demonstrated administrative gifts, spiritual maturity, leadership ability, and a genuine love for world missions.

Time Requirements
This position will require approximately two hours per week for the next twelve months.

Although all the student leadership positions are important, I've learned that the key student leadership positions for every mission trip are the Student Director and the Student Shepherd.

Student Shepherd

The Student Shepherd functions as the "pastor" for the trip. He or she is responsible for the spiritual focus of the experience. The Student Shepherd works to see that students are challenged in their walk with God as they carry out the missions project.

The Student Shepherd fulfills the following job description.

Student Shepherd

Primary Function
Create and monitor an environment for the spiritual growth, welfare, and unity of the First Church mission project team.

Responsibilities

1. Create a log and diary system for the mission project team.
2. Facilitate a nightly afterglow meeting at the mission project site.
3. Encourage, support, and care for the Student Director.
4. Build relationships with the mission project team prior to the trip to foster spiritual unity.
5. Handle interpersonal problems while on site.
6. Encourage and support the adult sponsors on site.
7. Create an encouragement system (e.g., Secret Pal, Barnabas Board) to promote spiritual unity and peer ministry among team members.
8. Provide a thought or verse for the day while on site.
9. Attend all mission project leadership meetings.

Supervision Received

Youth Pastor

Supervision Exercised

Mission Project

Qualifications

A high-school student who loves world missions, possesses administrative ability, and demonstrates the spiritual gift of faith.

Time Requirements

Approximately two hours per week for the next twelve months.

Team Directors

As much as possible, you want your students to own their own trip. They can learn to draft a timeline, make budgets, and run a publicity campaign. They're doing it at school. And the more responsibility your kids take for their own trip, the more God can be working in them as they are stretched by new challenges.

You'll want to set up your student leadership teams at this time. You may need teams for publicity, budgeting, transportation, fund-raising, prayer support, and logistics for your training meetings. The size of your group may make these "teams" as small as one or two kids; no matter. The more kids you have involved in making the trip happen, however, the better.

Each team has a Team Director who is responsible for leading that team in its specific responsibilities. The Team Director reports directly to the youth pastor.

Student Banker

The Student Banker is responsible for helping to develop the budgets and for managing the funds for the trip. He or she works hand in hand with the financial leadership of your church. The role of the Student Banker is explained in more detail in chapter ten.

Lines of Communication

The key to making student leadership work is the strength of your communication lines. The best way I've found to make this work is with a *phone chart*—a written chart that delineates how the lines of communication will work. The following phone chart is an example.

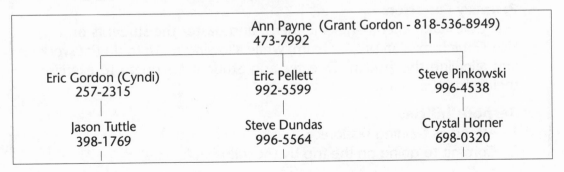

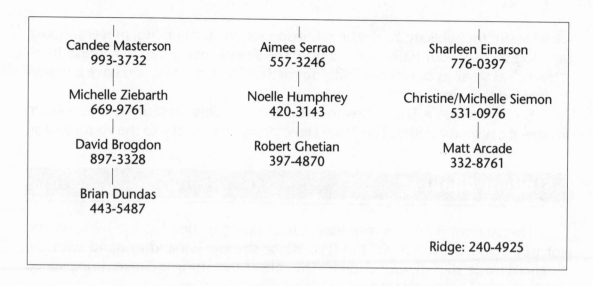

Candee Masterson 993-3732	Aimee Serrao 557-3246	Sharleen Einarson 776-0397
Michelle Ziebarth 669-9761	Noelle Humphrey 420-3143	Christine/Michelle Siemon 531-0976
David Brogdon 897-3328	Robert Ghetian 397-4870	Matt Arcade 332-8761
Brian Dundas 443-5487		

Ridge: 240-4925

Adult Coaches

Under the supervision of the Student Director and the Student Shepherd is a team of adult coaches. The term "coach" serves to remind the adults of their role in the mission trip.

The adult coaches operate under the following job description.

Adult Coach

Primary Function

Train, facilitate, encourage, shepherd, and pastor the students on the First Church mission project team, while allowing them to do the work and allowing the Student Director and Student Shepherd to exercise their leadership roles.

Responsibilities

1. Attend all training sessions.
2. Commit to going on the trip by (deadline date here).

3. Commit to a regular time of involvement with the high-school group this year, including attendance at the winter retreat.
4. Attend the monthly mission project staff meeting.
5. Fulfill tasks as requested by the youth pastor (e.g., renting vehicles, cooking, assisting in medical emergencies, etc.).
6. Coordinate on-site discipline in cooperation with the youth pastor.
7. Encourage the students on site.
8. Facilitate site manager/student leader communication.

Remuneration
First Church will pick up all direct expenses (e.g., transportation, food) related to participation in the mission project.

Qualifications
A Christian man or woman who genuinely likes high-school students and has had some experience working with them. He or she should have a flexible lifestyle, an encouraging temperament, an optimistic outlook, and a servant's heart.

The coaches facilitate the work to be done rather than doing the work themselves. The challenge is to find adults who can allow kids to be participants rather than spectators. This is a lot more difficult than it sounds. The tendency for most adults is to take charge, particularly when they are with a group of kids.

I remember a mission trip we took to Mexico City a few years back. Anticipating the possibility of frequent breakdowns with our church bus, we recruited Joe, an experienced mechanic, to drive the bus from Los Angeles to Mexico City. Miraculously, the bus made it most of the way down before we had our first catastrophe: a major blowout on the right front tire. Joe sprang into action. He got the bus off the road, got the kids off the bus, and went to work.

It didn't take long to see that Joe was the only one working on the bus. In fact, he seemed the only one concerned with getting the tire changed at all.

Some of the kids were playing frisbee and others had changed into their swimming suits to jump into a nearby river. Joe was getting madder and madder. He was having trouble changing the tire and he needed help. But I wanted the kids to take ownership in the situation, so I coaxed Joe, over his protests, to a nearby *tienda* for a soft drink.

There was one student on this trip who did not fit in with the rest of the group. He sat in the back of the bus and said very little. When he spotted Joe and me in the *tienda*, he came in and sat with us. "Hey," he said, "I noticed that nobody's working on the bus." He asked whether he could help change the tire. Joe was shaking his head "no" when I began asking the kid more questions. It turned out that his father owned a tire store, and he knew exactly how to change a bus tire, even on a "suicide rim" like the ones on that bus.

When I gave the kid the go-ahead, he bounded out of the *tienda* and got to work, Joe and I trailing behind. In no time at all, he had that rim flying, the tire off, the tube in, and the new tire on. He even put the air back in the tire with a bicycle pump, which was all we had.

By this time the other kids had surrounded him, cheering him on. He had gone from geek to hero. From that point on, that kid was totally different. He served as one of the student leaders on the following year's mission trip.

Developing Your Mission Statement

The first thing you'll work on with your Student Director and Student Shepherd is the development of a trip mission statement. Have them create a three- to four-sentence statement describing the purpose of the trip. A mission statement could read like this:

The First Church mission project is a missions education project for high-school students designed to emphasize the gifts of service and helps. The project will give our students a firsthand experience on the mission field. We also hope the mission project will develop solid leadership potential within the youth group by providing active leadership roles for our students.

This statement provides the framework for the goals, objectives, and plans you will subsequently formulate.

Using your mission statement, work up twenty prospective goals for the trip. These will provide a wonderful point of discussion for your regular meetings with your student leadership.

You, your Student Director, and your Student Shepherd should do a first draft of your prospective goals separately. Then, come together and distill your worksheets down to the goals that will serve as the criteria for your mission trip.

Your goals might look something like these.

First Church Mission Project Goals

1. Link all student leaders with a national pastor for communication and planning purposes by November. All correspondence will be done in Spanish.
2. Recruit two other churches to join our mission project.
3. Make the mission project a line item in next year's church budget.
4. Secure all adult leadership for the mission project by October.
5. Have each student write a three-page paper on the culture of the people we'll be ministering to at the mission project site and turn it in by December.
6. Take the mission project student leadership on an overnight planning retreat in January.
7. Have every student and adult participant "adopt" a child at the orphanage in our mission project site by March.
8. Have a church elder participate as an adult coach on the mission project team.
9. Provide a solid leadership link between the Student Director, Student Shepherd, site directors, and adult staff.

10. Have the chairman of the church missions committee visit the missions project site when the group is there.
11. Produce a quality, stimulating, and challenging worship experience for the mission project while on site.
12. Keep a daily journal of thoughts about the mission project. Include such entries as personal feelings and observations about participants.
13. By May, host an evening social/mixer to bring the adult coaches and student staff together.
14. Maintain accurate financial records.
15. Involve the senior pastor in the missions project as much as possible. Ask him to join the team on site.

Once you have agreed on your goals, ask the students to write down all the tasks necessary to accomplish those goals. This list can easily contain up to two hundred different tasks.

For example, you'll need a publicity plan to recruit kids for the trip. A publicity plan can include producing flyers and brochures, making presentations to the youth group, the parents, and the church at large. Although this is a painstaking process, it allows your kids and you to see exactly what needs to be done to make the trip a reality.

Setting Up Your Master Plan

After you've drawn up your list of tasks with your Student Director and Student Shepherd, schedule an all-day planning meeting as soon as possible with your larger student leadership—your youth council, mission trip committee, or whatever grouping of students you'll want to be in charge of the trip. Calculate how much time is available between now and the start of your trip. Then, take the list of tasks your students have developed and determine when each task needs to be done. As you decide, place them on a master trip calendar. For example, if you want your students signed up for your trip by April 1, you will need to have your applications out by March 1. This means that you'll need to have your applications written and printed by late February.

This long-term planning helps you avoid putting off tasks until too late and gives you your agenda for your ongoing trip planning meetings. The following Project Serve timeline gives you an example of such a plan.

Project Serve Timeline

January

1	Select all student leaders.
6	Finalize all goals and objectives.
13	Plan all fund-raisers and training. Discuss, decide upon, and contact helpers for publicity.
20	Secure all adult coaches. Select training dates. Begin discussion on daily schedule.
27	Finalize Project Serve leadership seminar.

February

3	Finalize daily schedule and training. Discuss and write. Meet with adults.
10	Finalize trip guidelines. Select slides and write script for slide show.
17	Meet with adult leaders. Complete Project Serve brochure mock-up.
24	Complete fund-raising plans. Finish training manual. Select Curriculum Committee.

March

3	Discuss and decide upon speaker. Secure speaker. Confirm by letter ASAP. Finish sound track for slide show.
10	Inform church elders. Write application.
17	Finalize all publicity and media. Print training manual. Discuss menu. Contact rental agencies. Finalize assignments for training program. Write permission slip.

24   Finalize application. Present VBS curriculum plan. Develop format for student journals.

31   Distribute applications. Evening parent meeting; discuss parent involvement plan.

April

14   Project Serve Sunday. Secure all transportation. Hold parents' briefing. Contact insurance agent. Order shirts. Finalize curriculum.

21   Applications due. Menu final. Secure all rental equipment. Receive all permission slips. Conduct team interview and selection process.

28   Announce teams. Form phone chain. Finalize insurance. Announce prayer partner sign-ups.

May

5   Finalize crafts. Print student journals. Finalize chapel plan. Begin prayer partner sign-ups.

12   Plan trip debrief. Print shirts. Form parent prayer groups. Secure border clearance. Contact doctor regarding medical kit. Enlist parental leadership. Schedule meeting for prayer groups.

19   Secure interpreters. Have student leaders form afterglow plan. Finalize trip logistics list.

26   Secure prayer partners. Deliver modesty talk to youth group. Plan departure Sunday.

June

2   Finalize afterglow plans. Pot luck!

9   Purchase supplies. Secure medical kits. Pack VBS materials, crafts supplies, etc.

16   Project Serve departs!

Keeping Track of the Details

Although we want students to be responsible for the trip, we need to remember that we're working with busy high-school students who will need consistent reminders of what they've decided. One way we've addressed the issue is by jogging our kids' memories with copies of detailed minutes from every planning meeting held.

Reprinted here are minutes from an actual Project Serve planning meeting held in November, 1986, when I was serving as youth minister at Wheaton Bible Church. I'm reprinting the minutes in their original form to give you a clear example of how specific, and helpful, such minutes can be.

Project Serve Planning Meeting

November 14, 1986

The Project Serve meeting was held on November 14, 1986, in the Wheaton Bible Church Board Room.

Present: Tom Stoner, Sue Bolhouse, Ridge Burns, Thom Day, Tim Onufrock, Megan Kelly, Kris Jordan, and Lynnaea Heck.

Absent: Erin Ash

I.   The meeting was opened in prayer by Ridge Burns.

II.   We discussed scheduling for the Project Serve student leaders' planning meetings and decided on the following dates:

December 15 & 22
January 23 & 26
February 9 & 23
March 8 & 22
April 5 & 12
May 10 & 24
June 7 & 14

III. Transportation to the sites.* We've received the following quotes for ground transportation to New York:
Keeshin Busline—$162 per person, round trip
Coach Travel Unlimited—$111 per person, round trip
Royal American—$180 per person, round trip
Amtrak Train—$170 per person, round trip
Midway Airlines—$320 per person, round trip
Monarch Coaches—$85 per person, round trip
It was decided to use Monarch Coaches as our prime source of transportation. Before signing a contract, Thom Day, and Tim Onufrock will personally inspect the buses we will be using. Tom Stoner has begun to research airfares for New York/Dublin and New York/Barcelona.

IV. Ridge read a letter from our contacts at the site in Ireland and expressed concern over the potential obstacles to conducting effective spiritual ministry in Ireland.

V. The following timeline was established:

January

1
- All transportation will be secured and contracts signed.
- All artwork for logos, T-shirts, etc., will be agreed upon and delivered from the artist.
- A Project Serve publicity plan will be finalized that will include publicity to our church as a whole, the youth group, and the community.

February

1
- All ministry sites will be finalized.
- Work projects for all ministry sites will be organized and designed.

* Project Serve sent out several teams each summer, thus the multiple sites.

March 1	• All fund-raising plans will be finalized.
	• All training plans will be finalized.
	• The student application will be finalized.
	• All food preparations will be finalized.
	• All passports will be in hand.

April

1
- A plan to involve parents in Project Serve will be finalized.
- The spiritual ministry components for each trip will be finalized.
- The team for each site will be selected.

June

1
- A debriefing plan will be finalized.

VI. The following key dates for Project Serve were established:

March

18 Project Serve Information Sunday (applications distributed; parents' meeting held that night).

April

1 Applications due.

7 Project Serve teams selected.

8 Project Serve teams announced to the youth group.

29 First training session and Project Serve fund-raising Sunday (a fund-raising campaign for the month of May will be explained to the congregation).

June

15 Parents' pot luck.

16 All luggage at the church to be packed on bus.

17 Project Serve teams depart.

July

15 Project Serve ministry report at the evening service.

VII. We discussed Christmas Project Serve. We will be working with Inner City Impact for approximately two and one-half days over the Christmas holidays.

VIII. Tim Onufrock shared a desire to take a member of a Chicago-area gang who has become a Christian to New York to serve as a cultural guide for the Project Serve ministry teams. We discussed the strengths and weaknesses of this idea and unanimously agreed that Tim pursue the idea with Dave Parker of Youth Guidance. Tim will report his findings at the next meeting.

Respectfully and messily submitted,
Lynnaea Heck

One of the students kept the minutes. She was also responsible to see that the minutes were typed, printed, and mailed to the youth group and to their parents. Allow your kids to take the responsibility to accomplish these things. It builds their self-confidence and prepares them for the even greater responsibilities they'll have on the trip.

You're now ready to move on to one of the most important components of the preparation process: selecting your ministry site.

9

Selecting a Ministry Site

HOW DO YOU GO ABOUT selecting a ministry site? How can you ever sort out all the possibilities? The key is in deciding *what* you want to do before you decide where you want to go.

For example, you may want your kids to focus on meeting physcial needs. In that case, it would not be a good idea for you to get involved with an overseas evangelistic crusade. It would be better to link with a rescue mission, soup kitchen, or home-building ministry.

Once you've determined the criteria for your site, you'll want to gather information on possible sites from a number of sources. Your most obvious source is your own church's missions committee. They know the missionaries your church supports, they know what those missionaries are doing, and they may be willing to put you in touch with them.

If at all possible, link up with missionaries who are supported by your church. They will have a greater interest in you and in helping your trip to be successful than an independent missionary might. It's also an opportunity for your students to see your church's missions budget up close and personal.

The Exploratory Letter

Your next step, after assembling a list of possible ministry sites, is to send a letter to the contact person at each ministry site outlining what you'd like to do on the mission. Your letter could read something like the following.

November 30, 1999

Rev. Mike Mission

Route A, Box B
Somewhere, Someplace

Dear Rev. Mission:

Having some familiarity with your work through our church, I am wondering if you might be able to help me. I am working to get our senior high students more involved in ministering to others, and in that regard, we hope to do some type of service project in the summer of 1992.

Could you make use of a team of ten to fifteen teenage young people (supervised by four adult sponsors) for a week of ministry? We could perform general maintenance work—painting, simple repair, basic construction—or put on a Vacation Bible School or other children's ministry.

We will pay for our own transportation and food, and we will pay for at least part of the supplies needed if we complete a work project. We ask the host group, if possible, to provide a place for us to sleep, and a place for us to prepare our food.

We have strict selection criteria for our students. They must apply to be accepted for the trip, and those accepted undergo extensive ministry training. You can be assured that we will bring you teens who have committed themselves to the project.

I hope to hear from you soon. If you feel such a project can be of assis-

tance to your ministry, we can begin to work out the details immediately.
If you have questions, please do not hesitate to write or call.

Sincerely Yours in Christ,

John Doe

Minister of Youth

Research as many potential ministry site options as possible. Not every lead for a mission trip will work out. You may have to make as many as fifteen to twenty contacts to come up with two to three viable ministry sites.

Even after choosing your site, keep one or two possibilities in reserve, in case you run into unforeseen problems. I was all set to take a high-school team to a ministry site in Central America one summer when that country's government was overthrown in a violent coup. A few phone calls from anxious parents made it clear that there would be no trip to that country. Fortunately, I had another option that I was able to pursue, and we had a wonderful mission experience that summer.

Your Site Manager

Although the site itself and the ministry opportunities available there are important, the essential ingredient for a successful ministry site is a missionary at the site who will look after and really care for your group. I call this person the Site Manager.

Many times, short-term youth mission teams are more work than help for the missionaries. In searching for the right Site Manager, you need to find a missionary who sees your trip as more than just extra work and hassle for him or her. This missionary will be someone who believes in short-term mission exposure as one of the tools God uses to call his servants. This kind of a missionary will be eager to work with your group and will give your students an authentic taste of missionary life.

I've developed a job description that I send to potential site managers to give them a clear idea of what I'm hoping they will be able to do for our group.

Site Manager

Primary Function

The Site Manager is directly responsible for the relationship of the First Church students and the sponsoring organization at the site.

Responsibilities

1. Helps our students to understand the culture in the ministry site area.
2. Serves as liaison between the existing ministry at the site and First Church.
3. Prays for our group before, during, and after our time on the site.
4. Orients our students upon arrival, including tips on cultural awareness, safety precautions, guidelines for behavior, and setting up the basic logistical and functional policies.
5. Arranges pre-arrival logistics.
6. Helps to keep us from making mistakes that will hurt the ongoing ministry at the site.
7. Encourages the students while on site.

Site Inspection

The idea of site inspections can be daunting. They're time-consuming, expensive, and can generate criticism (as in, "Why is the youth pastor trotting all over the world on the church's money?"). But I cannot overemphasize their importance. The ministry site described by letter, phone, or even personal interview can turn out to be radically different than what you discover when you see it for yourself. If you commit to a mission site without checking it out beforehand, the results could be disastrous.

In 1986, we were planning to take one of our Project Serve teams to Ireland. Everything sounded great as we began making our arrangements. Through our letters and phone calls, it appeared that we were headed for a wonderful ministry site. It wasn't until I went to see the site that I realized we would have problems. The community the kids would be ministering in was too legalistic, and there was not enough work for them to do. Upon arriving home, I canceled that ministry site and we arranged for an alternate site.

Beyond making sure that the ministry site is actually what you understand it to be, your primary goal on a site inspection is to gather as much essential information as you can. The following questionnaire can serve as a model.

Site Inspection Questionnaire

Date _____

Project _____

Address _____

City _____ State _____ Zip _____

Country _____ Postal Code _____

Telephone _____

Preferred Team Size _____

Minimum Number Accepted _____

Location
1. What is the population of the area?
2. What language is spoken in this area?
3. What is the current political situation in the area?

Weather
1. What is the climate usually like on the dates we plan to be there?
2. What is the elevation of the ministry site?
3. Will weather be a factor for our team when they're on site? If yes, what specific weather issues will they face?

4. Does the team need to bring bug repellent?
5. What kind of clothing is recommended?

Church/Mission

1. What is the name of the church or mission?
2. How many attend the church or mission?
3. What is the membership of the church or mission?
4. When was the church or mission organized?
5. How involved will the local church members or mission members be with the project?
6. Will the church or mission contribute financially or with other resources (e.g., building materials, supplies) to the project? If so, how much?
7. What are the primary needs of the congregation/mission?

Ministry opportunities

1. What type of ministry will we do at the site (e.g., construction, general repair, children's ministry, Vacation Bible School, door-to-door evangelism, food distribution)?
2. If this is a building project ministry, are building plans drawn for the project? When will building plans be sent to team coordinator?
3. What skills are needed for the project?
4. What tools or equipment should be brought by team for this project?
5. What do we need to be aware of if we attempt to clear customs with tools?
6. What is the electrical voltage? 110- ___ 220- ___ cycles? ____
7. Will there be opportunities to preach/testify?

Transportation

1. To what city would the team fly?
2. What transportation is available from the airport to the site?

3. How much will this transportation cost?
4. What kind of transportation will be needed daily to get to the site? How much will it cost?

Housing
1. Where will our students be housed?
2. How many beds are available?
3. Will we be paying rent? If so, how much per person per night?
4. How far will the housing be from the ministry site?
5. Are there sleeping arrangements for couples? If yes, how many couples can be accommodated?
6. Will kids need to bring any of the following? (Check all that apply):
   ☐   Sleeping bags or cots
   ☐   Bed linens
   ☐   Towels and washcloths
7. Which of the following facilities are available? (Check all that apply):
   ☐   Showers
   ☐   Hot water
   ☐   Nearby river
   ☐   Toilets with running water
   ☐   Outhouse

Food
1. What food is availble in the area?
2. Is additional food available in adjacent areas? If so, where? How far are these areas from the ministry site?
2. What, if any, food items does the team need to bring?
3. What are the average costs in the local restaurants for
   breakfast: _____ lunch: _____ dinner:_____?
4. Is there a supermarket, an open market, or both?
5. How does the cost of food compare with the U.S.?
6. Is there safe drinking water available?

7. Is there pure ice available?
8. Describe the cooking and dining facilities (stove, refrigerator, pots and pans, silverware and dishes).
9. What, if any, utensils does the team need to bring?
10. Describe the laundry facilities.
11. What is the cost to use the local laundry facilities?
12. Does your mission station provide a package that includes travel, food, and housing? If yes, how much is the fee per person per day? What does the fee include?

Communication/Safety

1. Is there a telephone at which a team member can be reached in case of emergency? What is the number?
2. Is there a phone nearby from which a team member could call the U.S.? What is the number?
3. Is there messenger service? If so, what is the address for the messenger service?
4. If there is no phone or messenger service, how could a team member be contacted in case of emergency?
5. Where is the nearest hospital? What medical services are available there?
6. How far is the nearest doctor from the ministry site?
7. What are our options if we encounter a medical emergency?

Entering and leaving the country

1. Is a passport required?
2. Is a visa required? If yes, where is it secured? What is the cost? What documents are required?
3. What inoculations are required? What inoculations are recommended?
4. Is there an airport entrance tax? How much? Exit tax? How much?

5. What specific things should be said and NOT be said when going through customs and immigration?
6. What should be put on the visa application as to the purpose of the visit?
7. What location and address should be put on the visa for "Place of Residence" while in the country?

Finance
1. What is the name of the local currency?
2. What is the exchange rate between the local currency and the U.S. dollar?
3. How should U.S. dollars be brought into the country (e.g., traveler's checks, cash, other)?
4. Does this country require each individual to exchange a specified amount of U.S. dollars into local currency at the time of entry into the country? If yes, how much?
5. Will each individual have to declare the amount of dollars he or she is carrying at customs and immigration?

Clothing
1. What is appropriate dress for women:
   On site?
   While touring?
   At church?
2. Are slacks permissible for women:
   On site?
   While touring?
   At church?
3. Are women required to wear hats when attending church?
4. Are sleeveless dresses permissible?
5. What is appropriate dress for men:
   On site?

While touring?
At church?
6. Are men permitted to work on the job without shirts?
7. Will there be opportunity for swimming?
8. What specific cultural sensitivities should the team be aware of?

Sightseeing
1. What are the local areas of interest?
2. How much do they cost to visit?
3. How far are they from the ministry site?
4. How much would transportation to the local places of interest cost?
5. Are there local stores that sell souvenirs?
6. How do prices compare with the U.S.?

Miscellaneous questions
1. What specific items could the team bring to help with the local ministry?
2. What specific items could the team bring for witnessing?
3. What personal items would you recommend team members bring?
4. What personal items would you recommend team members NOT bring?
5. How can the team members best prepare themselves for this project spiritually?

Take time during your site inspection to build relationships with the Site Manager, the local people, the pastor of the church, the folks who will help you accomplish the things that God has called you to do on your mission trip.

If at all possible, take your Student Director and Student Shepherd with you when you go. It's a wonderful opportunity for them to gain information about the trip, and your time together on site will solidify you as a team. This is important enough to justify the expense, even if it means boarding an airplane. If you can't take your student leaders with you, have them contribute questions to your site inspection questionnaire. And when you're on site, try to put yourself in your students' shoes as you look things over. How would they feel about being there? What kinds of growth opportunities are there for them?

When you've confirmed your ministry site and returned home, it's time to dig into the nuts and bolts of your trip preparation. 🌴

10

Nuts and Bolts

NOW THAT YOU'RE EXCITED and your student leaders are excited about a missions trip, it's time to get down to the work of spreading the excitement to the rest of your youth group and to the church at large. To do this you need to generate publicity. After you get their attention with some creative publicity, it will be time to get approval for the trip, develop your budget, and raise money.

Publicity Plan

Your publicity plan, like all aspects of your mission trip, should be built around student leadership. Your student leadership can help to develop the publicity plan, oversee the production of the publicity pieces (mailings, brochures), and supervise the execution of the plan. And rather than make the initial presentation about the trip to the youth group yourself, have your Student Director and Student Shepherd do it. Following the presentation, make it a requirement for your student leadership to call all the members of your youth group and personally invite him or her to participate on the trip. There is nothing more powerful than one student calling another student to invite them on such a trip. Your student leadership can also lead the presentation to the parents at the Parent Information Day outlined in the following publicity plan.

We drew up the following publicity plan for one of our Project Serve trips. It can serve as a model for you as you design your own.

First Church Mission Project Publicity Plan

Enlist prayer partners

1. Have each trip participant sign up two people in the church who will commit to pray for that participant on a weekly basis prior to the trip, and on a daily basis during the trip.
2. Have the mothers of trip participants commit to meeting together for a special time of prayer while the group is on site.
3. Have trip participants try to get their brothers and sisters to commit to praying for them daily while the group is on site.
4. Have the parents/guardians of each trip participant commit to a special time of prayer together for their child while the group is on site.

Promote awareness of and involvement in the trip among church members

1. Have the youth pastor, Student Director, and Student Shepherd write an article for the church newsletter about the upcoming trip (complete with pictures!) when they return from site inspection.
2. Create and produce a bulletin insert about the trip to be placed in the church bulletin once a month for four consecutive months.
3. Write an announcement for applications and place it in the church bulletin each week for the four weeks prior to the application deadline.
4. Write and send a letter to all church members and regular attenders to make them aware of the trip and encourage their support.
5. Plan a special church service during which the church can be made

aware of the trip, kids can share their hopes and concerns for the trip, prayer partners can be identified and recognized, and the church as a whole can commit the group and the trip to God.

6. Have the youth group make a short announcement one Sunday in every Sunday school class.
7. Paint and place a sign advertising the trip in front of church (like you do with a VBS sign) for the three months prior to the trip.

Promote awareness of and support for the trip among the parents of trip participants

1. Hold a Parent Information Day no later than two months prior to your trip.
2. Provide parents with basic logistical information about the trip: when, where, costs (show slides you took on your site inspection).
3. Have your student leaders give a report on their hopes and expectations for the trip.
4. Moderate a question-and-answer session for the parents.

Promote and recruit for the trip within your youth group

1. Appoint a materials committee from your group to create, produce, and distribute the following materials according to your trip timeline.
   - Promotional poster
   - A pre-sign-up flyer
   - Trip brochure
   - Student application form
   - Parent/guardian permission forms
2. Schedule a student-led mission trip promotion night.
   - Have your Student Director and Student Shepherd do a presentation on the trip (show slides you took from the site inspection and artifacts/souvenirs from the area).
   - Go over your vision, hopes, and expectations for what the trip will accomplish for your group.

- Pass out trip brochure, student application forms, and parent/guardian permission forms.
3. Mail an additional set of one trip brochure, student application form, and parent/guardian permission form to every student in your group.
4. Have the kids in your student leadership committee divide up the group and personally call everyone in your youth group to invite them to participate in the trip.

Final Approval for Your Trip

There will come a point in every mission trip when you'll need to get the official approval of your church leadership for the trip—the missions committee, youth committee, elder board, or whoever in your church holds the authority. I have found it effective to have my students personally present the trip to the leadership for approval. To be honest, it's harder for the elders to say no to a student than it is to us! And I've discovered that the direct interaction between young people and the church leadership can be life-changing.

One year I asked a girl to draw a picture of the elders of the church before she went in to the meeting. She drew a picture that resembled the cover of a Dutch Masters cigar box—stoic old men with robes and long white hair. She was surprised when the elders of the church proved to be warm, energetic, and excited about the trip. She was overwhelmed when the elders gathered around her and prayed for her leadership.

After you've obtained the approval of the church leadership, have your students make an appointment with the senior pastor. When you meet, simply have your kids ask your pastor to pray for them. It's so encouraging for your senior pastor to pray with those students and hear firsthand what God is doing in their lives. Suddenly the senior pastor is not just that person who preaches on Sunday morning; he becomes a friend who's concerned with the lives of the kids in his church.

Budget Time

Finances can be the biggest struggle of any mission trip—not only raising the funds, but accounting for the funds. The best way to alleviate potential difficulties is to have your Student Banker sit down with your church treasurer and plan a budget for your mission trip based on the same format that the church uses. When your Student Banker and church treasurer work together, they will form a relationship that will help you present and report the financial aspects of your trip in a format that will make sense to the church.

Although your church may have a particular format it uses for budgeting, I've included the following budget worksheet for reference.

First Church Mission Project
Budget Worksheet—Air Trip   p. 1

	Cost Per Person	Number of Persons	Total
TRANSPORTATION			
From church to airport	_____	_____	_____
Round-trip airfare	_____	_____	_____
Visa fee (if any)	_____	_____	_____
Tips for baggage carriers (per bag x number of bags	_____	_____	_____
Between housing and ministry locations ($ per day x number of days)	_____	_____	_____

First Church Mission Project
Budget Worksheet—Air Trip

	Cost Per Person	Number of Persons	Total
Sightseeing: Transportation and Entrance fees	_____	_____	_____
From housing to airport	_____	_____	_____
From airport to church	_____	_____	_____
Layovers:			
Sightseeing	_____	_____	_____
Food	_____	_____	_____
Motel	_____	_____	_____
Transportation	_____	_____	_____
Other	_____	_____	_____
FOOD AND HOUSING			
Food per day x number of days	_____	_____	_____
Food brought from home	_____	_____	_____
Housing: Cost per room x rooms need for x days	_____	_____	_____
Laundry	_____	_____	_____

First Church Mission Project
Budget Worksheet—Air Trip

	Cost Per Person	Number of Persons	Total
Other (please specify)			
Package Fee* * For trip arranged through mission or agency that provides a package fee for housing, food, materials, local transportation			

MISCELLANEOUS

Administration (phone, correspondence, publicity, etc.)			
Materials not covered by separate budget or fund-raising			
Adult coach expenses not covered by separate budget or fund-raising			
Less free air tickets given by travel agency as part of group package			
Insurance			
Other (please specify)			
Less funds already budgeted for trip from youth budget, missions budget, or other source			

First Church Mission Project
Budget Worksheet—Air Trip

	Cost Per Person	Number of Persons	Total
TOTAL			_____
Divide by number of people on team		_____	
Cost per person	_____		

Getting Your Funding

The fact that we have to raise significant money for a mission trip can keep us from getting involved in student mission trips in the first place. However, raising funds for a mission trip is often surprisingly easy.

There are three main sources for funding: the church budget, parents and other interested individuals, and the students themselves. I try to set up a plan where one-third of the funding is raised from each source.

Church Budget

Often, your church's missions committee is struggling to promote youth involvement in missions and is more than happy to help with the funding if you can supply the kid power.

The best way to approach your missions committee is with a missions trip prospectus. This is an outline of the project that includes a purpose statement, budget, and other relevant information. I've printed below a sample prospectus (minus budget) from one of our Project Serve summer missions efforts:

Prospectus for Project Serve

Purposes for Project Serve

Project Serve is a missions education project for high school students designed to emphasize the gifts of service and helps. Project Serve gives high schoolers a first-hand mission and service experience. Furthermore, Project Serve seeks to develop leadership potential within the youth group by providing students with active leadership responsibilities.

Objectives for Project Serve

1. Expand Project Serve into family ministry by providing an all-family Project Serve experience.
2. Increase whole church involvement in Project Serve. We hope to be a part of raising the missions consciousness of Wheaton Bible Church. We are not as interested in promoting Project Serve as we are interested in promoting missions as a whole.
3. Give our kids direct contact with Wheaton Bible Church missionaries in order to build relationships between the home base and the field.

Student Leadership

Although Project Serve is directed by the director for high-school ministries, it is produced and run by high-school students. Each ministry site will be under the leadership of two key students: a Student Shepherd, whose responsibility is to create an environment that will foster team unity and spiritual growth; and a Student Director, who directs and facilitates the logistics for the ministry site.

The Student Shepherds for this year are:

Inner City—Erin Ash
Rural America—Kris Jorden

Foreign—Sue Bolhouse
Family Project Serve—Thom Day
The Student Directors for this year are:
Inner City—Tim Onufrock
Rural America—Linnaea Heck
Foreign—Tom Stoner
Family Project Serve—Thom Day

Projected Student Involvement

In a survey taken at the beginning of the school year, we asked students to indicate whether they are planning, Lord willing, to participate in Project Serve during the summer, over Christmas, or both. Seventy-one students indicated interest in the summer Project Serve; forty-one students indicated interest in Christmas Project Serve.

We project that sixty kids will participate in summer Project Serves, thirty-five in Christmas Project Serve, and ten families in the August Family Project Serve.

Ministry Sites

The following sites have been approached and are in varying degrees of confirmation for Project Serve:

1. Inner City—a team will work with Henry Sanchez in Brooklyn, New York. Henry runs a church and a community center in Brooklyn and also is involved in a camp approximately two hours from New York City. Our students will be involved in Vacation Bible School and community outreach projects and also will assist with the camp ministry. We expect twenty-five people at this site.
2. Rural America—a team will work with Henry Moore at His Mansion in New Hampshire. His Mansion is a farm experience for transients from the Boston and New York areas. At His Mansion, they experience a Christian community designed to put their lives back together. Our

students will work in conjunction with the local Brethren Church as well as assist in physical projects at His Mansion; they will live with families in the area. We expect twenty-five people at this site.

3. Foreign—a team will work either in Ireland under the auspices of Ireland Outreach or in Spain with our church-sponsored missionaries, the Franks. Ireland Outreach is located in Charleyville, just out of Dublin. Ireland Outreach works with a correspondence Bible school as well as a school located on their premises. We will be involved in community outreach and will work with the children attending the school. The Franks are with Greater Europe Mission in Barcelona, Spain. We would assist the Franks with both a Vacation Bible School and a camp ministry. There are some issues that keep us from making a final site decision at this point, but we are praying for God's direction. We expect ten people on the site.

4. Family Project Serve—a team of families will travel to the Tennessee-Kentucky area to work with Christian Appalachian Project. We will be involved in a Bible school ministry as well as some home construction. Christian Appalachian Project provides students and families like ours opportunities to serve the Lord through physical labor and spiritual ministry. We expect ten families on the site.

5. Christmas Project Serve—a team will work with Inner-City Impact in Chicago. We will assist with both construction and tutoring. We expect thirty-five students on this site.

Upcoming Decisions

1. Elder approval for our objectives, plans, and financial budget for Project Serve.
2. Approval for a fund-raising campaign of a dollar a day per family in the month of May.

Summary

Although Project Serve is only ten months away, we are moving along well in our planning process. Excitement is already building for Project Serve. Your prayerful consideration of our request for budgetary support for Project Serve is deeply appreciated.

Respectfully submitted,
Ridge Burns
Director of High School Ministries

Friends, Parents, Countrymen

Although parents are often reluctant to shell out more money for another camp or youth program, they can be much more open to supporting a mission trip. And relatives and other interested friends are often happy to support a young person's participation. I usually have our students write personal letters to these people, telling them about the mission trip and requesting their support. I've made a standing rule that students cannot solicit funds directly from church members whom they are not related to or do not know personally. This prevents possible ill-feelings arising from church members who are "personally" solicited for support when they feel they have already contributed to the trip through their regular giving.

Student Fund-Raising

I strongly advocate that students raise at least one-third of the money on their own. It's important for our kids to have a significant personal investment in the trip, and working to raise some of the funding dramatically increases their investment.

Group fund-raisers not only raise money for the trip, but also develop group cohesiveness and team unity that cannot be achieved in other ways.

Appendix B gives a number of specific ideas for group fund-raisers. But great ideas notwithstanding, please, please don't take God out of the fund-raising process! We can become so immersed in the methodology of raising money that we forget that it's God who provides the money, sometimes in miraculous ways. What's wrong with holding special youth group prayer meetings to seek God's provision in raising funds? I've seen too many examples of major dollars appearing in unheard-of ways at the eleventh hour not to believe in miracles. Making God an intentional, primary part of the process both enables us to maintain a proper perspective on our fund-raising efforts and to stay open to the wonderful ways God might want to work in our midst.

11

Now Accepting Applications

WE'VE ALREADY DISCUSSED the importance of your mission trip being a student-led event. I've learned that the more we ask students to do, the more they will do. The more commitment we demand of our kids, the more they'll deliver. In that light we approach the application process. "Application process" means just that—kids must apply to be accepted for the mission trip. They are not automatically included simply because they can pay the fee. Ministry is a privilege, not a "given." Nowhere is the reality of that made more vivid than on a mission and service experience.

It is very important that you include on your application form all the necessary dates and deadlines that are required for your students to go on this trip. This helps students to plan their lives around the trip and also to know in advance what is required of them.

When you design your application form, you'll want it to contain the elements found on the following sample form.

First Church Mission Project
STUDENT PARTICIPANT APPLICATION FORM

Name _____

Address _____

City _____ State _____ Zip _____

Phone _____ Year in school _____ Sex: ___M ___F

1. Do you consider yourself a Christian?
   Yes _____ No _____
2. What are your expectations for the mission project?
3. What do you expect God to teach you through the mission project?
4. What do you think you can contribute, through God's help, to the mission project?
5. Of the activities listed below, check those in which you've had experience:

   ☐ working with children   ☐ door-to-door outreach
   ☐ drama   ☐ music/singing
   ☐ Vacation Bible School   ☐ speaking to groups
   ☐ simple carpentry   ☐ painting
   ☐ shingling a roof   ☐ window washing
   ☐ weather stripping   ☐ wallpapering
   ☐ electrical   ☐ plumbing
   ☐ tiling   ☐ insulating
   ☐ auto mechanics   ☐ other (please list)

Health and Safety Information

Father/Guardian's Name _____

Home Address _____

_____

Home Phone _____ Work Phone _____

Mother/Guardian's Name _____

Home Address (if different from above) _____

_____

Home Phone _____ Work Phone _____

1. Please list any allergies you have:
2. Please list any medication you are taking:
3. Do you have any medical conditions (such as asthma) that could affect your health and well-being while on the trip?

Reference Forms*

*Attach three of the following reference forms to each student application. This reference form is to be completed by an adult other than your parent or anyone associated with the First Church youth group. This form must be completed and returned to First Church by Monday, _____. You may use the self-addressed envelope to return it directly to the church. Please sign the waiver on each reference form before giving it to the person filling out the reference.

I hereby agree to waive my rights to see this form once it has been completed.

Applicant's Signature _____

Date _____

Reference form

Dear Sir or Madam:

We appreciate your willingness to take the time to fill out this reference form. Please be clear and honest in your answers. It will help both the applicant and the ministry at First Church. Thank you for your help!

1. What three qualities best describe this student?
2. Are there any weaknesses that may affect this student's ability to make a positive contribution to a mission trip?
3. How would you rate the student in the following areas?

	HIGH	AVERAGE	LOW
Cooperation			
Works well with others			
Leadership ability			
Reliability			
Motivation			
Disposition			
Emotional stability			
Concern for others			

Do you have any additional comments you'd like to make?

What is your relationship to the applicant?

Name _____ Date _____

Phone _____

You will need a signed medical consent form from the parent or guardian of every student going on the trip, such as the one found below.

Suggested Medical Consent Form*

We, the undersigned, are the parents, the parents having legal custody, or the legal guardians of _____, a minor, and have given our consent for him or her to attend a mission project being operated by First Church. In the event that he or she is injured while attending the project and requires the attention of a doctor, we consent to any reasonable medical treatment as deemed necessary by a licensed physician. In the event treatment is called for, which a physician and/or hospital personnel refuses to administer without our consent, we hereby authorize _____, Director of High-School Ministries, or _____, Site Leader, to give such consent for us if we cannot be reached by telephone at one of the numbers indicated below or, because of an emergency, there is not time or opportunity to make a telephone call. In the event it becomes necessary for that person to give consent for us, we agree to hold such person free and harmless of any claims, demands, or suits for damages arising from the giving of such consent so long as the treatment is administered by or under the supervision of a licensed physician.

Telephone Numbers: _____ _____ _____

_____ _____

Signatures: (show relationship to the student)

_____ Relationship _____

_____ Relationship _____

Date: _____

· **Note: Have this, or any other medical consent form you use, checked by your church lawyer or other qualified legal representative before putting it into use.**

Trip Guidelines

Written guidelines for appearance and behavior should be passed out with the student applications. The guidelines should be complete, specific, and strict. The higher the standard we call our kids to, the higher the standard they will strive to attain. Your guidelines could look something like these, which were drawn up by my high-school students at the Wheaton Bible Church.

First Church Mission Project
GUIDELINES

Appearance

1. Slacks and jeans are to be worn for travel and casual wear. Shorts can be worn only by permission of the Team Leaders.
2. T-shirts with messages on them can often be offending. Do not wear T-shirts with sexual messages or advertisements, T-shirts advertising alcoholic beverages or tobacco products, or any message that you think may be offensive.
3. Dress modestly. No tight clothing (shorts, pants, T-shirts, etc.).
4. Sunday dress for girls should be skirts and dresses; dress shirts and slacks for guys. No jeans.
5. Thick-soled shoes, not sandals, are to be worn while at the work site.
6. When coming to the breakfast table, your hair should be combed and you should be dressed for the day's work.
7. If you will appear before people before going to bed, be sure to wear a robe.
8. Our guidelines for appearance are designed to be sensitive to local cultural standards. Complaining about what we can or cannot wear is unacceptable. We are a part of a different culture; we adapt to what is appropriate to our hosts.

Behavior

1. Be positive and flexible. The success of the ministry depends on your attitude. Ask God to keep you in a right frame of mind.
2. Watch your language. Swearing or off-color jokes will not be tolerated. Be particularly careful about gossip.
3. Stay out of arguments. No matter how much you disagree, come to a mature resolution.
4. Never make negative comments about the food.
5. "Lights off" means we are quiet and going to sleep. Our effectiveness depends on how much rest we can get.
6. We want you to have fun while working at the mission project site. Be careful, however, about excessive goofing off on your work site.
7. Be on time. Your lack of regard for our schedule can disrupt the entire team.
8. Treat the facilities as if they were your own. Do not vandalize any facility. If an accident takes place, please notify your Team Leader so that we can make appropriate restitution to the facility owner.
9. Be friendly toward the people you come in contact with. Learn their names and include them in your conversations.
10. Show interest in what you are doing and in the people at and around your site.
11. Pick up after yourself. Your messiness can affect the morale of the whole team.
12. Use good table manners at all times. Guys should allow the girls to get their food first.

Relationships with authority

1. Respect all your adult and student leaders. Obey their instructions. Your Student Director and Student Shepherd have the authority to direct the team. They have prayerfully considered their roles and are praying for you.

2. Obey all cultural rules.
3. The Bible tells us that if there is a problem, you are to go to the person you have the problem with first. If you cannot come to a mature resolution, go to your Student Director or Student Shepherd and allow him or her to help you work things out. Do not discuss your problems with other members of the team. That is gossip.
4. We welcome any constructive critiques. Please direct your critiques to the adult and student leaders.
5. Never leave your site without permission. Always let your leaders know where you are going.
6. The only way our mission project will work is through your continued daily devotions and personal prayer.
7. Encourage your adult and student leaders. They sometimes feel lonely and left out of the team.

Relationships with fellow team members

1. Be sensitive not to leave other team members out of your activities or conversations. Do things together and try your best not to develop cliques.
2. Do not be a loner. Work with others, and communicate your impressions, hopes, joys, and frustrations.
3. Do not cause others to feel unwelcome or unwanted by telling secrets or private jokes in front of them.
4. Interpersonal conflicts can become aggravated in a high-stress environment like a mission project. Be patient with other team members. Do not hold grudges.
5. Concerning boy/girl relationships, the following rules apply:
   a. No holding hands, heads on shoulders, sitting on laps, back rubbing, sitting with special boyfriends or girlfriends on buses or at meetings.
   b. Our purpose in participating on the mission project is to serve

the Lord, not to establish romantic relationships. Seek to guard yourself from making that the focal point of your week.

   c. If you are part of a couple, make a promise to reach out and extend yourselves to other members of the team.

Miscellaneous Do's and Don'ts

1. No alcohol is to be consumed on the mission project. This includes ministry in cultures where wine is commonly served at all meals.
2. No nonprescription drugs are allowed on the mission project.
3. No smoking, tobacco chewing, or snuff dipping.
4. Do not bring any radios, tape recorders, Walkman™ radios, or cassette tapes.
5. *Never give your home address to anyone while on the mission project. Give the address of the church.*

Training Camp

For the mission trip to be successful, your successful applicants, before they depart, must be trained for the specific tasks they will need to know. This training process is what distinguishes many mission trips from other forms of youth programs.

First, they need to be trained in the **logistics of the trip**—how to cross a border, how to go through customs, how to fill out a landing card on an airplane, how to fill out a visa, how to exchange currency, how to get and take care of a passport, and other essentials.

They also need **cultural training**. One of the worst things we can do to kids is to send them into another culture without teaching them how to be sensitive. I remember a group of kids I took to Mendenhall, Mississippi, a few years ago. We were sorting clothes down at a thrift shop in the black section of town. Each morning we walked from the gymnasium where we slept to this thrift shop. The neighborhood was almost always deserted of cars, and our kids got into the habit of walking as a group down the middle of the street. It was a novelty for our kids, raised in an auto-glutted suburb, to be able to walk down the middle of a street.

The last day of our trip, I went to one of the local leaders of the program for an evaluation of how our group did during the week. After paying us many compliments, he smiled and said, "I'm a little hesitant to tell you this, but the people in our town are a little bothered that your kids walk down the center of the street like they own the place." A simple thing like walking down the street was a cultural issue, and we were needlessly offensive. Chapter five lists sources for simulation games you can use in your pretrip training to help your kids gain cultural sensitivity.

Third, your kids will need ***ministry training***. They'll need to understand and learn some simple phrases in the language of the area where you're going, how to work with children, how to break the ice with an older person, and construction training, if you're planning a building or repair project.

One year we committed to build cinder-block houses in Tijuana. Before we went, we arranged for a skilled mason who attended our church to take us to one of his work sites and let our kids practice how to lay block.

Finally, your kids will need ***interpersonal training***. Unlike camps or retreats, mission trips, with their high levels of unfamiliarity, insecurity, and cross-cultural stress, require a tremendous amount of mutual support and trust between the team members if the trip is to be successful. The preparation sessions outlined in chapter six, particularly the Team Covenant exercise in session one, are designed to help you foster mutual support and team unity.

No Show, No Go

Training sessions and information meetings should be "no show/no go," unless there's a legitimate reason for a student to be absent. Let the kids know this at the beginning of the application process. Then, if a student has a conflict with one of the dates, he or she can make note of it on the application form.

I also strongly recommend that you keep all of your deadlines firm. If you begin to make exceptions, you'll find it more difficult to foster a spirit of accountability when you're actually on site.

Getting the Whole Church Involved

Getting your whole church behind the mission trip can be a blessing for everyone. A youth mission trip can unite the entire congregation around a central purpose. I recently preached in a church where a group of laypeople were leaving to serve in a refugee camp in Honduras for a week. The pastor invited the entire team up to the platform for a prayer of dedication and commission. When the pastor finished his prayer, the entire congregation gave them a standing ovation. This team of short-term missionaries had captured the imagination of their own congregation, and it was a beautiful thing to see.

There are several ways to get your whole church involved. The first is through prayer partners, where each kid on the trip is being prayed for by at least two members of the church (as described in the Publicity Plan in chapter ten). Have your students take the addresses of their prayer partners with them on the trip and write their prayer partners a letter from the field. Encourage the prayer partners to write or call their students before the trip. It's a powerful thing for a student to get a call from an adult saying, "I'm praying for you as you go on your mission trip. I'm anxious to hear what God will do."

Sending You Off in Style

Arrange for your church to hold a commissioning service the Sunday before you leave for your trip. It's a powerful experience of worship and support for both your kids and the congregation. I've always scheduled my mission trips to depart right after the Sunday morning worship service. This way, our church members are the last people to pray for the kids as they take off.

We would become the choir on such a Sunday morning. Later, the elders and pastors of the church would gather around the students and dedicate them for ministry. Then, the entire church would move out to the lot where our vehicles were parked. The congregation would gather around those vehicles and offer a prayer of dedication and safety.

We would also communicate with our church during the mission trip. We would send two-minute cassette tapes that could be played over the loudspeaker on Sunday morning. The church got a firsthand account of what God was doing on the trip. We would also set up a "communication center"—someone in the church whom we would call every day with a report from the field. That person then took calls from anyone in the church who wanted an up-to-date report of what was happening on the mission trip.

This link between the kids and your church is a tremendous boost while preparing for your trip. It's a link you can nurture during your time on the field, and, after you return, it can strengthen the bond between your youth group and the congregation at large. 🌴

12

On Site

YOU'VE FINALLY MADE IT to your ministry site. If it's your first mission trip, it can be overwhelming—so many new sights, smells, and situations. What to do first? What to watch out for? What's it really going to be like?

Every mission and service trip has its distinctive trials and blessings. Every schedule is different. But there are some similarities; and the following suggestions and tips should help you maximize your time when you're in the field.

Keep a Daily Schedule

Given the distinctiveness of each mission and service trip, schedules can vary widely. But the following daily schedule can be used as a guideline for your own planning.

First Church Mission Project
DAILY SCHEDULE
   Morning
   Get up.
   Breakfast (30 minutes).

1. Review schedule for the day.
2. Have an encouragement exercise to build team unity.
3. Go over any special assignments, such as kitchen crew or water detail.

Personal devotions (25 minutes).
1. Time in solo devotions.
2. Time with a devotion partner.
3. Time in devotional prayer.

Ministry instructions for the day (10-15 minutes).
> Cover specific instructions for your ministries, e.g., VBS, construction, children's ministries, work crews

Morning ministry.

Afternoon

Lunch and rest time (1 hour).
Afternoon ministry.
Personal/free time for kids; staff meeting for student and adult leaders (1 hour).

Evening

Dinner.
Cultural education/presentation.
1. Local speaker.
2. Touring the area.
3. Other.

Debrief.
1. Singing/worship.
2. Sharing what God did that day.
3. Prayer.
4. Writing in journals.

Lights out.

Tips for Success

Don't worry, be flexible. Mission and service trips could be called God's answer to Murphy's Law: Everything that can go wrong will go wrong. Supplies are misrouted, communication is garbled, and expectations are misunderstood.

I took a group to Columbia to build a bathroom for a local church. We'd arranged for the construction supplies to be waiting for us when we arrived on site. They were there, all right—but at the bottom of a steep hill, at the top of which sat the church. It took us two full days just to carry the supplies up to the work site before we could begin construction.

Although there's no substitute for careful, thorough planning, it's wise to go into a mission and service trip with an attitude of flexibility. Logistical complexities, differences in cultural priorities, and just plain unforeseen circumstances are often the norm rather than the exception. But this is also one of the great benefits of a mission and service experience. When we're forced to set aside our own expectations and trust God for the here and now, amazing things can happen.

One year our group was on its way to Honduras to run a Vacation Bible School. Our plane made a stop in Belize on the way—and I do mean stop! As we touched down on the runway, the landing gear broke and we skidded to a halt. No one was hurt, but we were informed by the airline that we'd be laid over for two days—and that we were on our own while we waited. This "airport" was in the middle of a cluster of rural villages, basically in the middle of nowhere.

We tried to figure out what to do. Should we take a bus to Honduras? Try to arrange for another plane? Nothing was working out. Then our kids had an inspiration. We'd come to run a VBS; if we couldn't do it in Honduras, we'd do it there. They set up their crafts, puppets, and story circles and held a VBS right there at the airport! Word spread quickly, and within a few hours the airport was filled with children from the nearby villages. It was a wonderful two days of ministry.

Give your kids the chance to encounter God. One of the dangers of a mission project is that we can become so obsessed with completing the project that we forget why we went in the first place. Although those we minister to do appreciate our efforts at repairing their church roof or building a bathroom, most cultures other than ours value relationships more than things. "Pastor Von" Trutz-schler has often said that he arranges construction projects primarily to keep the Americans happy while he's building relationships with the local people.

There are ways we can ensure that our kids will have regular opportunities to grow in their relationship with the Lord while on site. A regular time of singing and worship each day, keeping a personal spiritual journal, and getting time alone for focused devotions will help kids to maintain their spiritual base. One thing I've found helpful is to give the kids a word for each day as a focal point for their thoughts and prayers. Words such as *patience, confidence, joy, obedience, trust, servant-hood, commitment*, and *others* can serve as reminders of why they're there as they journey through the week.

Build in unstructured personal time each day. Everyone has a certain need for privacy and quietness. The cramped quarters and group living of a mission trip create their own stress. Be sure to program some time each day for kids to write letters, nap, talk, or just relax.

During our week-long Center for Student Missions camps in inner-city Los Angeles, we designate four to six o'clock every afternoon as free time. One group started an Uno game that continued throughout the week! The chance to unwind together every afternoon proved to be the tonic they needed to offset the stresses of the week.

Provide a place where your adult leaders can get a break. Adults, even more than kids, have a need for privacy and space. Set aside an area, no matter how primitive, as an "Adults Only" space—a place where your adult leaders can rest, write, pray, and just relax. Giving your adults the chance to get away regularly while on site will keep stress levels down and leader effectiveness up.

Work hard, then play hard. I don't believe in mixing work and play during a mission trip, lest our goals get confused. At the same time, people need a "sabbath" day that's devoted to unfettered rest. I've found it effective to concentrate on the work at hand for a solid period of time. When that's completed, our kids can then enjoy their day off with clear minds and a sense of accomplishment.

Fun days should be that—fun. And with a little creativity they can be a unique addition to the trip. One year we took our kids to Brooklyn for two weeks. When the kids first arrived, they were planning an off day built around visits to the usual New York sights—the Statue of Liberty, the Empire State Building, Central Park, and so on. But as the first week progressed and our kids began to build relationships with their peers in the neighborhood, a new idea emerged: Why not get a tour of the city through the eyes of the locals? The neighborhood kids loved playing host, and our group was treated to a unique view of the city they never could have experienced on their own.

Meet with your staff daily. Gather with your Site Manager, Student Director, Student Shepherd, and adult leaders to touch base about the week. Take time to take stock, celebrate joys, address any problems that have arisen, and brainstorm about ideas. It's both a great way to keep tabs on the progress of the week and deepen the bond within your leadership team. The following outline gives you an example of items you can cover during your daily staff meeting.

First Church Mission Project
STAFF MEETING

1. Time of prayer for:
   - Specific people.
   - The ministry.
   - Each other.
2. Who do we need to especially encourage?
3. What equipment and/or supplies do we need to obtain?
4. Review tomorrow's schedule.
5. Hear from the Site Manager:
   - How our group is doing.
   - Any problems to address.
   - Suggestions for greater effectiveness.

Encourage your kids in creative ways. Your kids will need regular doses of encouragement throughout the trip. There are several ways to keep this happening. Pair your students off with prayer partners they can meet with each morning to share and pray. Set up a "Barnabas Board"—a simple bulletin board or plywood wall where your kids can write notes of encouragement to each other. During one or more of your evening debriefs, hold an "affirmation circle" where, one by one, each kid has the chance to be personally and specifically affirmed by the other students. And I've found that a communion service the last morning or evening of the trip is a powerful time of worship, bonding, and closure.

Keep your kids culturally sensitive while on site. After a few days on site, the cultural sensitivity the kids brought with them begins to wear off. To keep them aware and sensitive, have a time each day to remind your kids of where they are and how God wants them to relate to their surroundings. Bringing in a local speaker to encourage and challenge your kids can be very effective. I've also found that taking a "prayer tour" through the area (walking if the location is rural or small, driving if it's urban or spread-out) is a great reminder. Another way to keep your kids culturally sensitive and to inject variety into the schedule is to take public transportation, rather than your own vehicles, to your ministry site.

End each day with a time of singing, worship, and debriefing. Your group times together each evening are crucial opportunities for your team to focus on God and what he is doing in this mission. Spend time just praising the Lord in song and prayer. Have your students share with each other about what God is doing in them. Help your kids focus on God, not on themselves, as they share.

This is a time when you can have your kids make entries in their student journals. They can set down their feelings, write out prayers to God, and even draw "mental snapshots"—pictures that describe what God is doing in their lives and hearts. The kids can share their journal entries if they wish.

Your debriefing time also gives you the opportunity to help your kids understand their experiences in the context of your trip goals. You can help to interpret the events of the day—what went right, what went wrong, the joys and struggles your group experienced—in light of God's larger purposes.

He is Faithful

It's impossible to fully understand how God can work through a mission trip until you've actually experienced it. As you maintain an attitude of flexibility, trust God for the everyday details, and nurture your team's relationships, you will be stunned by how quickly God will mold your bunch of diverse (and sometimes difficult!) individuals into a body of believers, focused on his service. And you will be surprised at how deeply God digs into your own heart as well. 🌴

13

Homeward Bound

CONGRATULATIONS! You've just returned from an amazing week of ministry, safe and sound—if more than a little tired. It's time to drop off the kids, return your vehicles and equipment, throw your clothes in the washer, take that much-needed shower, and collapse for a well-deserved rest. Right?

Well, not quite. Although you'll no doubt want to build in time for some R & R when you return home, there are two follow-up steps you can take that will multiply the impact of your trip: a post-trip presentation to your church and an evaluation of your experience.

Post-Trip Report

It's a great boost for your church members when your kids can tell about the fruits of the church's investment of money, time, and prayer. But one of the dangers of these post-trip presentations is that the exciting experiences in the

Lord these kids have had can fall flat in the presentation. The kids either tighten up in front of their own church or they get so emotional that the adults can't figure out what the kids are talking about.

An effective way for kids to share their experiences is to have each one bring back a physical symbol from the trip that represents what God has done in his or her life. This symbol can be as simple as a rock or bark off a tree, or it can be as complex as a garment handcrafted by someone at the site, or even something the kid made while on site.

One student brought back a Confederate flag from our Mississippi trip. He explained that before he went on the trip, the flag represented a cute southern symbol, something stock car drivers put on their cars. He went on to say, "I now realize that this is a symbol of hate and prejudice against some of God's children. I don't want that in my life." He then produced a Bic lighter and set the flag on fire. It was a powerful statement of his desire to remove bigotry from his life.

On another trip, a football player brought back a vial full of water. He then went to his high-school football field, got a little bit of dirt, and put it in a plastic bag. He stood up in front of the church, held up his symbols, and said, "This dirt represents the most important thing in my life when I'm at home—football. This water represents the thing that changed my life this summer—this mission trip. I want these two things to work together so that I can play football for God." As he talked, he poured some water into the dirt. He held up the mud and said, "This is what I want to be in God's hands, pliable and used in his service."

Evaluate Your Trip

If you're really serious about creating mission and service experiences that will help your kids grow in their faith, you need to thoroughly evaluate each trip: How well did your system work? What did you learn on site that will help you improve future trips? Did you achieve your intended purposes on the trip?

Go back to the goals you originally developed and evaluate how you did in reaching those goals. The following sample evaluation form can serve as a model.

First Church Mission Project
Student Evaluation Form

Please rate the trip using the following scale: 1 = Needs Work; 5 = Awesome

Comments

Did the trip provide a realistic missions experience? 1 2 3 4 5

Food: 1 2 3 4 5

The Ministry sites I was at:

_____ 1 2 3 4 5

_____ 1 2 3 4 5

Site manager: 1 2 3 4 5

Adult coaches: 1 2 3 4 5

Student leaders: 1 2 3 4 5

Youth minister: 1 2 3 4 5

Preparation for the trip: 1 2 3 4 5

Schedule while on site: 1 2 3 4 5

Spiritual impact of the trip: 1 2 3 4 5

Overall experience: 1 2 3 4 5

What was the most positive aspect of the experience?

What was the most negative aspect of the experience?

How would you suggest we improve the experience?

Would you participate in another mission trip? Why or why not?

Make the results of the evaluation available for the church leadership, the missions committee, and the parents. Include an addendum to the evaluation results that summarizes how the money was spent and what the bottom-line profit or loss was from the trip. The large amount of dollars invested in a mission trip makes providing this kind of accurate accounting a must.

Finally, get together with your Student Director, Student Shepherd, and Student Banker. Take them out for a nice dinner to help them celebrate what God has done and to say thanks for their hard work. Give each of them a personal memento of the trip, such as a photograph of the team on the ministry site, with a personal note from you.

At this celebration dinner, give them the opportunity to do an informal postmortem of the trip. Then pick their brains for suggestions for future Student Directors, Shepherds, and Bankers. Give them the chance to select next year's leaders.

It always surprises me whom they pick. They don't necessarily pick the obvious leaders or the most popular kids; they pick kids who have a servant's heart and really love the Lord, people they know will do a good job. I've found that in most cases, the students are better judges of character than I am because they know exactly what it takes to lead other students. It's a powerful and wonderful time of celebration and passing on the mantle of leadership.

They're Rounding the Turn and . . .

You've now brought your kids through the process of investigation. They've become aware of God's vision for mission and service, and they've been immersed in a challenging, adventurous mission experience. In the next section, we'll discuss the final stage of mission involvement: integrating a commitment to mission and service into their lives at home. 🌴

Section 4

Back at the Neighborhood Pool

14

Serving in Your Own Backyard

REMEMBER THE MYTHICAL KID I mentioned in chapter three—the one who will someday come up to you and ask, "How can we use at home what we've learned on mission trips?" Well, that young person has arrived in your youth group. You're ready to integrate mission and service into your youth ministry at home.

Like your mission trips, you'll want your home mission efforts to be student-owned and led. Students too often lose a sense of ownership over local mission projects because, at the first sign of crisis, adults (like us!) bail them out. Our kids need to know that without their participation and leadership, the ministry will in fact fail. There is nothing wrong with a program bombing for a few weeks if it helps kids to learn responsiblity and to experience consequences of their inaction.

Six Ways to Bring It Home

Here are six ways you can involve your kids in long-term home ministry.

Help with a Meals on Wheels program. Meals on Wheels programs provide low-cost food for elderly people who are unable to prepare meals on their own. Your kids can make meals in their own church kitchen and then deliver them along a specific route. You could get involved on a daily or weekly basis, or you could serve as a substitute, which usually means that you're responsible for two meals a month. Check your local Meals on Wheels office for details as to how you can be involved. Meals on Wheels is a national program and can be contacted through either the United Way or the United Way Volunteer Bureau.

Work with the homebound. In every church there are people who are unable to get out of their homes, even for church services. One youth group in Atlanta divided the shut-in population of their church into seven groups. They then got high-school volunteers to pastor each one of those seven groups. Each elderly shut-in in those groups receives a phone call every day from a high-school pastor-encourager. The young person chats with the shut-in, finds out if he or she has any problems that need to be taken care of, and asks if there is anything that the church can provide for that person. This daily contact with the outside world is a wonderful source of encouragement for a homebound person.

Work with a local rest home. As our national population ages, more and more rest homes are opening up. Although these homes provide the elderly a good place to live and a certain amount of companionship, they are often terribly lonely places. Your kids can have a powerful ministry with the people who live in these homes.

Rather than trying to provide a program or going in to mingle as a group (two methods that usually lead to quick burnout), assign each kid to two or three residents. Each student can then build an in-depth relationship with "their" two or three people without all the pressure of preparing a program or trying to get acquainted with everyone at the home. These relationships can be very rewarding for your kids as well as for the elderly people they visit.

Volunteer on a community hot line. Hot lines can be a practical way to get your students involved in reasonably nonthreatening counseling situations. After the short training course that most community hot lines offer, your students can staff phone lines where they can work with kids struggling with drugs and pregnancy and other difficult issues. Check with the hot lines in your community for their policies on using teenagers.

Tutor children. Have your kids serve as tutors for children from the local grade school. Most school districts are desperate for productive after-school activities for the thousands of latchkey kids in their charge. Tutoring provides such an activity and can be a great outreach to the local school children.

Work with latchkey children. The explosive growth of the latchkey population is one of the major social stresses in modern American culture. In addition to tutoring children, there are other ways to get your kids involved in this vital ministry. There are after-school programs offered by local school districts, the YMCA, Boy Scouts and Girl Scouts, and other organizations that are in need of volunteers. Some youth groups are beginning to do their own after-school programs. One girl in my youth group at the Wheaton Bible Church had a vision for an outreach to latchkey kids right in our backyard that became a miraculous example of what kids can do when they respond to God's call to live out their faith at home: Sidewalk Sunday School. 🌴

15

Sidewalk Sunday School: A Home-Grown Missions Model

EVERY DAY AFTER SCHOOL, between four and six million children under the age of 10 come home to an empty house or apartment. The phenomenon of "latchkey" children, as they are commonly called, has become one of the most pressing social issues of our time.

Latchkey kids are found in every cultural, ethnic, and economic level. Whether they're in single-parent or dual-income families, the parents of these children face economic pressures powerful enough to force them to leave their children alone and unattended for several hours each day. These parents fear for their kids' safety, struggle with guilt, and try to parent in absentia over the phone. It's a situation tailor-made for stress, danger, and abuse.

Wheaton, Illinois, is known for its many Christian organizations and its attractive, expensive homes. Yet less than two miles from the church where I served as youth minister there are pockets of high-density housing where the income per household averages between $8,000-$12,000 per year. These are not welfare housing projects; they're apartments filled with refugees from around the world, low-income whites, and single-parent families.

It was in one of these high-density complexes that we began an ongoing weekly ministry called Sidewalk Sunday School. Sidewalk Sunday School was born out of the process we've discussed throughout this book—bringing high-school kids through the stages of mission involvement to the point where they desire to integrate mission and service into their lives at home. Over eight years, our Project Serve mission trips had sent high-school students all over the world. This steady exposure to God's vision for his people worldwide cultivated a hunger in a few key students to replicate their mission experiences at home.

Through Sidewalk Sunday School, our high-school students experienced cross-cultural mission work in their own backyard. The project was initiated, directed, funded, and administered by high-school students in the student body at Wheaton Bible Church.

The apartment complex where they began Sidewalk Sunday School housed a mix of cultures: low-income whites, Hispanics, Asians, and American blacks. This diverse mix provided an incredible cross-cultural experience for our students. It was common for our kids to remove their shoes when entering an apartment to honor the culture of the family to whom they were ministering. Kids hauled out their high-school Spanish books to help them communicate with parents and kids.

I'm convinced that the Sidewalk Sunday School can, and needs to be, replicated throughout the country. The handbook we developed to inform other interested churches about the Sidewalk Sunday School concept is reprinted here for your use. We hope that you too will catch the excitement for this ministry.

The Sidewalk Sunday School Handbook

I. Vision Building

Any idea worth doing must be able to accurately communicate its God-given vision. In the case of Sidewalk Sunday School, this communication involved direct steps that are transferrable to any group that would like to start a Sidewalk Sunday School ministry.

We had a student with vision. Sue Bolhouse, then sixteen years old, was the girl with the vision. Sue had her heart broken for these people. Once her heart was broken, she was ready to transfer her vision to her peers. High school students listen to high school students. Sue became the spokesperson for Sidewalk Sunday School.

We investigated the vision. We called the local police chief and asked him for the location of the housing complex with the greatest concentration of latchkey children. We then talked to the rental agency for that complex and found out what some of their needs were. We began to talk with some of the residents. We called the County Health Services Office and the schools to get as much information as possible on this complex and the people who lived there.

We provided a biblical base. In our large-group meetings and small-group ministries, we began to teach about widows, orphans, and the responsibility we have as Christians to lighten the load. Over time, we made students spiritually aware of this need.

We committed to regular prayer. Sue and I prayed for the vision that

God was building in our kids' hearts and asked him to spread it to the whole high-school group.

I checked my own heart. Someone said, "You can only take your students as far as you've gone." It wasn't until I had shed tears over the plight of latchkey children that I began to catch Sue's vision.

II. Ownership

It was one thing to have the youth pastor and one student excited about this new project, but now it was our task to excite the entire student body and get them involved. We took the following course of action.

We shared the cause. On Sunday mornings, we would tell about the families our students would be in contact with at Sidewalk Sunday School. We told of cases of child abuse, broken homes, and malnutrition that were taking place just one and one-half miles from our church. Gradually, students began to get more and more sensitive to the needs around them.

We got specific. We began to talk about the concept of Sidewalk Sunday School—going out to the complex each day to work with these latchkey kids. We began to share information about how much the program would cost and how involvement in Sidewalk Sunday School would affect their lives.

We recruited. One Sunday morning, we asked kids to sign on the dotted line to get involved in Sidewalk Sunday School. We asked each of them to give two and one-half hours each week for three months.

III. Selection of Site

Once we had a firm commitment from our kids, we crystallized our goals and plans.

We determined what we could handle. With a high-school group of our size, we determined that we could handle sixty to seventy latchkey kids. If your group is smaller, you may want to limit the size of the area where you will minister. I know of a group of fifteen high-school students that runs a latchkey program out of a residential home.

We staked out a specific geographic area. We chose a specific apartment complex in neighboring Carol Stream. There are many complexes in the same area, but we decided to try to meet the needs of the "total person" in one complex. We believe that a central focus is one reason Sidewalk Sunday School is effective.

We organized our student and adult resources. Sue selected a student leader for each day that Sidewalk Sunday School was in operation. The directors were to supervise and motivate their own staffs. The diagram below illustrates how we organized Sidewalk Sunday School:

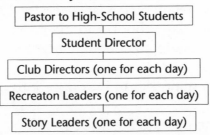

Pastor to High-School Students

Student Director

Club Directors (one for each day)

Recreaton Leaders (one for each day)

Story Leaders (one for each day)

We developed the following job descriptions for staff positions.

Job Description

Sidewalk Sunday School Student Director

Purpose

The purpose of the Student Director is to administer the Sidewalk Sunday School program for the residents of Greenview Lake Apartments.

Responsibilities

1. Develop and produce all curriculum materials.
2. Facilitate a weekly Director's meeting.
3. Keep the bulletin board up to date in the Sidewalk Sunday School apartment.
4. Provide activities such as movies, circus, films, etc.

5. Make announcements concerning Sidewalk Sunday School in student body meetings.
6. Coordinate crafts and song programs.
7. Recruit and train adult sponsors.
8. Facilitate sharing times after each Sidewalk Sunday School experience.
9. Keep staff morale high by giving variety to the program.
10. Publicize Sidewalk Sunday School to the church, and solicit the church's active prayer support.
11. Encourage strong relationships between the Greenview Lake complex, Sidewalk Sunday School, and the Wheaton Bible Church.
12. Provide and coordinate an adequate financial base.
13. Assist in staff recruitment.
14. Researching new ministries to introduce into the Sidewalk Sunday School program.
15. Provide adequate training for student staff.
16. See that the Sidewalk Sunday School apartment is properly maintained.

Time Commitment

Fulfilling the job of Student Director of Sidewalk Sunday School will require eleven hours each week, broken down as follows:
1. Three hours for the Sidewalk Sunday School program.
2. One and one-half hours for curriculum development.
3. One hour for building relationships.
4. One and one-half hours for meetings with Ridge.
5. One hour for a Director's meeting.
6. Two hours on the telephone.
7. One hour for staff recruitment.

Also, it is possible that in early fall, the Director's responsibilities will include going out to the site every day.

Sidewalk Sunday School Club Director

Purpose

The purpose of the Club Director is to facilitate the daily Sidewalk Sunday School program.

Responsibilities

1. Delegate the following tasks:
   a. Interest center supervisors (4)
   b. Storyteller
   c. Songleaders (2)
   d. Puppeteers (2)
   e. Outside recreation leaders (2)
2. Make sure there are at lest ten staff people on site. Call your staff to let them know times and tasks for the day.
3. You are responsible for the craft for your day. If possible, have the craft coincide with the story.
4. Meet individually with the Student Director once per week.
5. Attend two all-Club Director meetings per month.
6. Be familiar with the curriculum.
7. Facilitate prayer and share times before and after Sidewalk Sunday School.

Job Description

Sidewalk Sunday School Adult Sponsor

Purpose

The purpose of the adult sponsor is to facilitate and assist the student ministry of Sidewalk Sunday School.

Responsibilities

1. Drive the van to and from the apartment.
2. Encourage student staff by praying for them and assisting them if they are having problems with the children.
3. Help control the children during the story and the craft.
4. Demonstrate affection to the children at the complex.
5. Keep attendance (the Director will assist you).
6. Help set up the craft.
7. Supervise refreshments.
8. Pray daily and individually for the children you meet.

We raised the funds from the youth group. Sidewalk Sunday School has been totally funded by high-school students. We were amazed at how much money they were able to give. We operate on a $750 a month budget. This kind of ministry not only offers kids a new way to use their money, but provides a creative way to understand stewardship.

We dedicated the project. Once we picked a complex, organized our student leadership, and completed our training, we took the entire high-school group to the complex on Sunday morning. We traveled to the site in school buses, and there dedicated the project to God.

IV. Practical Considerations

Many practical considerations must be examined if a project like Sidewalk Sunday School is to be successful.

Insurance. Liability is of utmost concern. It takes a special insurance policy to cover the church's liability. Remember, your church is liable, not just you.

Permissions. Because we live in a cold-weather climate, we needed to rent an apartment in the complex to run a year-round program. The lease we signed prohibits religious activities. Therefore, we needed to get a special letter of permission from the landlord. This was a great prayer victory for the kids. Below is the text of our agreement letter:

We the undersigned agree that the Wheaton Bible Church will be holding "Bible study" type classes in 631 E. Gundersen Dr., Carol Stream #107 apartment at different times during the week. The undersigned acknowledges this fact and agrees that any liabilities that occur in the apartment are not to be held against Inland Real Estate Corp.

Legal considerations. Because we work with children, we needed to guard ourselves against any kind of suspicion. We hired a lawyer to advise us how to handle this issue. He gave us three suggestions: Have clear, written permission by the landlord to hold such a program in the complex; require each staff person to wear an identification badge at all times while on the complex; require the latchkey children to wear name tags while in the apartment. (Consult a lawyer in your area for additional suggestions.)

Authorization from your church leadership. Before we began Sidewalk Sunday School, we sought permission from the church leadership. We also asked them to sign the twelve-month lease we were committing to. Their willingness to risk along with us was a tremendous affirmation. It is crucial that you get approval from your church leadership before moving ahead with Sidewalk Sunday School.

V. Budget

Sidewalk Sunday School is a faith ministry. We ask our students to pledge money based on their ability to give. They respond through the offering envelopes we pass out each Sunday morning at our Sunday school class. We do no organized fund-raisers.

On a regular basis, we present a balance sheet that itemizes the financial condition of Sidewalk Sunday School at that time. Below is an example from 1984:

Sidewalk Sunday School Budget—October 1984

Rent	$4,788
Supplies	1,200
Postage	500
Printing	500
Summer Director	1,000
Total budget	$7,988
Giving through September 1984	$5,247
Funds needed by 12/31 to meet budget	$2,741

VI. Sidewalk Sunday School Daily Schedule

3:30 P.M.:	Staff meets at church to pray. Club director gives a thought for the day.
3:45 P.M.:	Staff arrives at complex, puts on name tags and buttons, and sets up interest centers (Sidewalk Sunday School has five interest centers—a playdough center, a storybook center, a household center, a building center, and a puzzle center).
3:55 P.M.:	Staff waits on street corner to meet school bus when children get off.
4:00 P.M.:	Recreational activities—checkers, card games, stories, art projects. Hold recreation outdoors when weather permits.

4:30 P.M.:	Singing. Use guitar if available. If it's not, go for it anyway.
4:50 P.M.:	Bible story.
5:05 P.M.:	Memory verse and craft time.
5:25 P.M.:	Closing prayer. Staff walks kids home and returns to apartment by 5:50.
5:50 P.M.:	Closing prayer session for staff.
6:00 P.M.:	Return to the church.

VII. Curriculum

We have used a variety of curricula, depending on the age group of the students who participate. Presently, most of our children are under the age of eleven, and we have found that the Character Foundation Curriculum, Early Childhood Kit, from Fleming H. Revell, Old Tappan, New Jersey, works best. The following is a sample curriculum plan:

Week One—Light

Day 1	Fun Fair
Day 2	Story: "God Created Light" Reference: Genesis 1:1–5 Craft: Color wheel
Day 3	Story: "I Am the Light of the World" Reference: John 8:12 Craft: Candles
Day 4	Story: "We are the Light of the World—Evangelism" Reference: Matthew 5:14–16 Craft: Sun pinwheels
Day 5	Story: "How We Should Act as Lights" Reference: Ephesians 5:8–10 Craft: Stars

Week Two—Water and Sky

Day 1	Story: "The Creation of Water and Sky"
	Reference: Genesis 1:6–8
	Craft: Boats out of Ivory soap
Day 2	Story: "Noah and the Ark"
	Reference: Genesis 6–7
	Craft: Rainbow
Day 3	SPECIAL ACTIVITY
Day 4	Story: "The Big Catch of Fish"
	Reference: Luke 5:1–10
	Craft: Fish pictures out of watercolor paints
Day 5	Story: "The Ascension"
	Reference: Acts 1:1–11
	Craft: Cloud pictures

Week Three—Land

Day 1	Story: "God Created Land"
	Reference: Genesis 1:9–10
	Craft: Open
Day 2	Story: Open
	Reference: Open
	Craft: Open
Day 3	SPECIAL ACTIVITY AT CITY PARK
Day 4	Story: "Rock and Sand"
	Reference: Matthew 7:24–27
	Craft: Sand jar creations
Day 5	Story: "Who Can Have Done This?"
	Reference: Matthew 13:14–20
	Craft: Sand jar creations (cont'd.)

Week Four—Vegetation

Day 1	Story: "God Created Vegetation"

	Reference: Genesis 1:11–13
	Craft: Terrariums
Day 2	Story: "Parable of the Sower"
	Reference: Matthew 13:1–23
	Craft: Seed collage
Day 3	SPECIAL ACTIVITY
Day 4	Story: "Consider the Lilies"
	Reference: Matthew 6:25–31
	Craft: Grass egg heads
Day 5	Story: "Fruit of the Spirit"
	Reference: Galatians 5:22
	Craft: Fruit mobile

VIII. Cross-Cultural Guidelines

Because we are going into a cross-cultural situation, we train our Sidewalk Sunday School staff to be culturally sensitive. In addition to using such resources as educational films and simulation games, we issue the following guidelines to all of our Sidewalk Sunday School staff.

1. Do not give your address or phone number to any resident of the apartment complex.
2. Wear your Sidewalk Sunday School badge at all times while on the Sidewalk Sunday School premises.
3. Do not display any signs or directions outside our apartment.
4. Do not enter any other apartment except the Sidewalk Sunday School apartment.
5. Be careful in your relationships with apartment residents of the opposite sex. No girl should talk to any guy without a Sidewalk Sunday School male staff person present.
6. Do not accept gifts from Sidewalk Sunday School participants. Do not promise to give or bring them anything from your home.

7. Be in prayer about Sidewalk Sunday School and ask God to use you to reach kids for Christ.
8. Our dress code is as follows:
   a. No sweat pants are allowed.
   b. No T-shirts with questionable advertising, rock stars, beer commercials, or sexual innuendos.
   c. Shoes always should be worn. No thongs or sandals are allowed.
   d. Girls should dress modestly. Avoid low-cut tops, blouses made of thin material, or tight-fitting clothing.
9. Avoid comparisons between our culture and the culture of apartment residents. Remember, we are guests in their neighborhood.
10. No more than twenty-one people may be in the apartment at any given time, and the back bedrooms are off limits.
11. No cars are allowed in the complex area. Transportation will be provided from the church.
12. Watch your talk, particularly around Spanish-speaking people. People often can understand far more than they can speak in another language. Therefore, always speak in an encouraging and loving tone.
13. Be friendly. Greet everyone you see, and be sure that people understand that they are welcome to our program.
14. Do not hang around each other. We are there to serve the people at the apartment complex.
15. Walk kids home only in pairs, never alone.

IX. The Different Programs
Tutoring Program

Linking with the local elementary schools, we provide a tutoring program for kids called "Homework Helpers." We focus on reading, math, and writing skills. Each one of our "Homework Helpers" goes through a six-week training period directed by one of the professional tutors in our church.

Library or Reading Club

We have developed a library of used children's book donated by church members. With these books, we have started a book club out of the Sidewalk Sunday School apartment. If students check out, read, and write book reports on at least thirty books, they receive a Sidewalk Sunday School T-shirt.

The Sidewalk Sunday School Sports League

Since Sidewalk Sunday School works primarily with kids under eleven years old, the junior-high age boys in the complex weren't part of the program and were starting to get into trouble. Now when the van comes to bring the Sidewalk Sunday School staff to work with the children, the van returns to our church gym with a group of junior high-aged boys.

Under the direction of a leader and some of our more athletic guys, the boys play basketball, indoor soccer, or floor hockey. Our older guys gain entry into the boys' lives and are able to present the claims and promises of Jesus Christ.

X. Church Relations

In addition to fostering ownership of Sidewalk Sunday School among the high-school group, we've worked hard to spread that sense of ownership throughout the church. The following programs have been most effective:

Food Drive

From time to time, we will ask church members to bring canned goods to stock a Food Pantry for some of the needy families in the complex.

Adopt a Child Program

Each one of our church families, if they desire, is given the name, address, and phone number of a latchkey kid. The family prays specifically for that child on a regular basis.

XI. In Summary

We hope you have found this handbook to be an inspiration as you consider launching a Sidewalk Sunday School ministry in your area. God bless you as you continue in his service!

Go Ye—With Blessings

It's been exciting to share this book with you. As you no doubt realize by now (especially if you read this book straight through!), leading kids into mission and service is the passion of my life. It's the ministry I've been called to, by God's grace. I just wish I could be with you as you take your kids through this exciting journey in faith and service. Go . . . with blessings!

Section 5

Resources for World Service

APPENDIX A

Bibliography and Resource List

Compiled by Paul Borthwick

Association of Church Missions Committees. P.O. Box ACMC, Wheaton, Illinois 60189. Helps churches develop missions resources and involvement. Their *Missions Education Handbook* offers excellent ideas on missions education for youth. Their "Bifocals" Bible study series also can be used in youth discipleship groups.

Borthwick, Paul. *Any Old Time - Book 5*. Wheaton, Illinois: Scripture Press, 1986. This addition to the Any Old Time series offers sixteen programs to help students reach out—according to Acts 1:8—to their own Jerusalems, Judeas, Samarias, and beyond.

_____. *How To Plan, Develop and Lead a Youth Missionary Team*. Lexington, Massachusetts: Grace Chapel, 1981. A short booklet for youth workers that answers the key questions about planning their own mission teams.

_____. *A Mind for Missions.* Colorado Springs: NavPress, 1987. Easy-to-read blueprint for building world vision. Offers ten building blocks to use in youth Bible studies or Sunday school.

_____. *Youth and Missions: Expanding Your Students' World View.* Wheaton, Illinois: Scripture Press, 1988. Explains how to motivate young people toward world missions.

Bryant, David. *In the Gap.* Downers Grove, Illinois: InterVarsity Press, 1979. A study guide proposing that God wants every Christian to be a world Christian. *With Concerts of Prayer*, by the same author, is also useful in encouraging people to pray for missions.

Campolo, Tony. *Ideas for Social Action.* Grand Rapids: Zondervan/Youth Specialties, 1983. Many ideas on youth involvement in outreach—fund-raisers, one-day work projects, work camps, and more.

Compassion International. P.O. Box 7000, Colorado Springs, Colorado 80933. A relief organization dedicated especially to the care of children. Their Compassion Project assists youth groups in promoting student involvement.

Everist, Norma. *Religions of the World.* Dayton, Ohio: Pflaum Press, 1979. A basic study that explains the contrast between world religions.

Fenton, Horace L. *Myths about Missions.* Downers Grove, Illinois: InterVarsity Press, 1973. Dispels your own and your students' stereotypes about mission work.

Fullerton, Fred, ed. *Youth Mission Education Leader's Guide.* Kansas City, Missouri: Nazarene Publishing House, 1987. Although written to inspire participation in their denominational missions, this volume is nevertheless useful in any church or youth group.

Give It Away. Book 7 in the Pacesetter Series. Elgin, Illinois: David C. Cook, 1987. Outlines for youth groups and Sunday school programs about outreach and missions, such as "What in the World Can Young People Do?" and "A Weekend of Service and Love."

Great Commission Handbook. SMS Publications, 701 Main St., Evanston, Illinois 60202. An annual of informative articles about short-term missions; includes listing of service opportunities.

Hinchey, Margaret. *Fund Raisers That Work.* Loveland, Colorado: Group Books, 1988. A myriad of ideas on raising money through youth group activities.

Howard, David. *Student Power in World Missions.* Downers Grove, Illinois: Inter-Varsity Press, 1979. Inspirational readings about the role young people have played in world evangelization, especially in our modern era.

Inter-Christo. 19303 Fremont Ave. N., Seattle, Washington 98133. A Christian placement organization that matches skills with positions worldwide.

InterVarsity Christian Fellowship. Box 7895, Madison, Wisconsin 53707. Producer of videos about missions, especially the addresses of "Urbana '87" (Inter-Varsity hosts the Urbana missions conference every three years) and the "To Every People" series.

Kane, J. Herbert. *Wanted: World Christians!* Grand Rapids: Baker, 1986. A guide to building your own vision for and involvement in the world.

Lupton, Robert D. *Theirs is the Kingdom.* San Francisco: Harper & Row, 1989. Wonderful stories of God's work in the city.

Mission Trip Planning Pak. Southern Baptist Convention, 127 Ninth Ave. N., Nashville, Tennessee 37234. An array of materials and ideas designed to help in the planning, fund-raising, and execution of a youth service team.

Olson, Bruce. *Bruchko.* Carol Stream, Illinois: Creation House, 1978. Fascinating, inspiring autobiography of a teenager who obeyed God's call to the mission field.

Operation Mobilization. P.O. Box 2277, Peachtree City, Georgia 30269. One of the largest organizations in the world for involving young people in world missions everywhere.

Richardson, Don. *Lords of the Earth.* Ventura, California: Gospel Light, 1985. Stirring missions biography that has enough action to hold a teenager's attention. Richardson's book (and film) *Peace Child* is also effective with young people.

Shaw, John C. *The Workcamp Experience.* Loveland, Colorado: Group Books, 1987. Pointers from the experiences of the leaders of *Group* magazine's workcamp program.

Stepping Out: A Guide to Short-Term Missions. Monrovia, California: Short-Term Advocates, 1987. A compendium of various issues related to short-term missions. Most useful for collegians or older.

Teen Missions International. P.O. Box 1056, Merritt Island, Florida 32952-1056. The champion of youth service teams, TMI sends out thousands of young people each summer in teams of twenty-five to thirty-five on six- to ten-week projects, virtually everywhere in the world.

Tucker, Ruth A. *From Jerusalem to Irian Jaya.* Grand Rapids: Zondervan, 1983. A biographical history of Christian missions. Contains an index of illustrations that is useful when preparing messages.

U.S. Center for World Missions. 1605 E. Elizabeth St., Pasadena, California 91104. A world-renowned resource center on missionary research that offers several publications through the William Carey Library.

Winter, Ralph, and Steven C. Hawthorne, eds. *Perspectives on the World Christian Movement.* Pasadena, California: William Carey Library, 1981. An encyclopedic volume on missions history, theology, and current issues. A valuable reference volume on missions.

World Christian. P.O. Box 40010, Pasadena, California 91104. A bright, informative, monthly magazine that helps readers understand and respond to the needs of missions.

World Relief Commission. Box WRC, Wheaton, Illinois 60189. The relief arm of the National Association of Evangelicals, WRC offers the fund-raising program Super Sweat for youth groups.

World Servants. 160 Harbor Dr., Key Biscayne, Florida 33159. Similar to Teen Missions International, but with more of a young group-building orientation. Offers short-term missions (two to four weeks) and encourages teams to come from the same youth group or church.

World Vision. 919 W. Huntington Dr., Monrovia, California 91016. A relief and development organization that has some great programs for youth group fund-raisers, including the "Love Loaf" program and the "Planned Famine."

Raising Money for Missions

There are six areas you want to address as you prepare to raise money for missions:

Help your kids develop a proper view of stewardship. One of the best ways to raise money is to ask kids to tithe their income. The average American high-school student makes $37 a week. If each kid would give $3.70 of his or her income every week to the youth budget, most youth groups would not have a problem funding their ministry. Set a giving goal for your youth group and keep your kids informed about reaching that goal.

Involve your kids in the fund-raising process. How many fund-raisers have you participated in where the adults did all the work and the kids did all the sitting? Have your kids take leadership in the car washes, bake sales, and rummage sales. It will build team unity and usually result in a better fund-raiser.

Make sure the return is worth the effort. Recently, a youth group in our area sold Christmas trees as a fund-raiser. The Christmas tree lot was open for

120 hours during the Christmas season. During each of those hours, at least two people were working. When they totaled up all the money they made and divided it by the number of people-hours they had put into the project, they made less than 50 cents an hour. They would have been better off if all the kids had worked at McDonald's for a month and given half their paychecks to the mission trip.

Ask. The biggest problem in fund-raising is our reluctance to come right out and ask for money. We do all these gimmicks to get people to the point of asking for money, but we're afraid to offend them, so we stop short. We need to remember that there are people who don't have time to participate on mission trips but gain great joy in financially supporting someone else.

There are two ways to raise funds: collect money or cut expenses. And there can be creative ways to do both. One youth group in Arkansas funded their mission trip by becoming the janitorial service for their church. The students clean the church, and the money that used to be paid to an outside janitorial service goes to the student missions fund.

Our adult ministries pastor once wanted to buy ten overhead projectors for $1,500. The church approved the purchase and included it in the budget. I thought that the local school district might have some overhead projectors they didn't need, so I checked with the district office. Sure enough, they had fifteen overhead projectors they weren't using and were happy to donate them to our church. I took ten of them to the adult education pastor's office. Placing them on his desk, I asked if he would be willing to transfer the $1,500 he had earmarked for overhead projectors to the youth mission budget, which he gladly did. It was a classic "win-win."

Don't leave God out of the process. With all of our gimmicks and clever ideas for raising money, we can forget that our source of funds is the source of all things. We leave God out of the process at our own peril.

Good Ideas for Raising Money

Mission Luncheons. After Sunday worship services, many people eat out, so why not serve a hot lunch in the church at a reasonable price? The members of one youth group served lunch four Sundays in May after church services. Parents were recruited to help. They prepared food such as barbecue chicken, slaw and salad, corn on the cob, hot rolls, tea, coffee, and dessert. It was an effective fund-raiser and helped to keep the mission trip in the minds of the congregation.

Windshield Wiper Brigade. A group of Texas high-school students raised funds for a local mission project with a "Windshield Wiper Brigade." Enthusiastic students, armed with clean rags and window cleaner, worked one Saturday afternoon at the parking lot of a large shopping mall. They placed colorful posters at the entrance of the parking lot. The posters said: "Help us find our way to the mission site. Let us clean your windshields for 25 cents each."

They got a tremendous response. The cleaning process took an average of one minute, and generous tips were offered to the workers to clean the chrome or dashboard. At the end of an extremely busy day, the group members found they had earned twice as much money as anticipated and made plans to work at other large parking lots across the city for future projects.

Fifties Drive-In. Turn your church parking lot into a "Happy Days" scene with a "Fifties Drive-In" fund-raiser. Offer hamburgers, hot dogs, fries, coffee, pop, and ice cream. Have gum-chewing, roller-skating carhops take orders and skate out the trays of food to customers. Use gas grills to prepare the food. Have your kids dress in fifties outfits: leather jackets, bobby socks, and greased hair. Give out free pieces of Bazooka bubble gum with each order, and have fifties music blaring.

By getting as many items as possible donated or purchased at a discount, you can earn a good profit and have a lot of fun.

Soup Sunday. Enlist the help of a church member who's known for good Italian cooking. Under his or her leadership, have your kids prepare a special Italian soup on Saturday.

On Soup Sunday, make a special announcement in church and ask three people who are considered the congregation's best cooks to come forward and sample the soup. These professional tasters will help attract a big crowd.

Charge a bargain price for a cup of soup and French bread, but make it clear that larger donations will be gladly accepted.

Buy a Mile. Members of a youth group in Oregon took a large colored sheet of poster board and sketched a map of their travel route to and from their mission site. They added up travel expenses and divided them by the total number of miles they'd travel. Using this cost-per-mile estimate, they drew a red line over their route to show how far they'd get on the money received thus far.

Church members were given the opportunity during the next few months to help advance the kids around the route by buying a number of miles. As money was received each week, the line was extended. This idea can both unify the church family in supporting the youth trip and provide a great visual picture of how the fund-raising is going.

New Year's Eve Baby-sitting Service. Looking for a good fund-raiser? Need a group activity for New Year's Eve? Combine the two! Announce in your church and community that your group is offering a super baby-sitting service for New Year's Eve. Set a price per child that will cover your costs and net your group a substantial profit. Have the parents drop their children off (with sleeping bags) at the church. They may pick them up the following morning.

Plan all kinds of fun stuff for the kids: games, movies, refreshments. When they have thoroughly exhausted your group, tuck them into their sleeping bags. Serve breakfast to the kids the next morning before the parents come.

Trash-A-Thon. Get pledges for every pound of trash your group can pick up in a day. The trash, and therefore the money, adds up quickly and this is one fund-raiser that requires a minimum of hassle and preparation. And your fund-raiser also benefits the local community.

"Uncommon" Stock Sale. This fund-raiser takes little preparation, yet can raise big money. The basic idea involves the word *investment*. The sales pitch goes like this:

> The recent history of the stock market has demonstrated how money can be lost in the market. Wouldn't it be refreshing to know that your money is invested in a certain winner? Forget "common" stock. Try buying our

"uncommon" stock instead. One hundred percent of the proceeds will be invested in materials to provide homes for the poor on our upcoming mission trip.

Sell the shares for $10 each. Besides your congregation, give local businesses, civic clubs, and private citizens the opportunity to invest wisely.

Christmas Post Office. Construct a box out of plywood, with little compartments large enough for letters and Christmas cards. There should be at least twenty-six compartments. After it's built, painted, and labeled, place it in a prominent place in your church, announcing that "The Christmas Post Office is now open." People are invited to "mail" their cards and letters to each other simply by placing them in the appropriate compartment and by paying 25 cents per card. Each week until Christmas, church members check the compartment with the first letter of their last name, and pick up their Christmas mail.

Drive-In Movie Night. If your church has a big parking lot, here's a great fund-raiser. Get a large movie screen and set it up on one end of the parking lot. If you have a building adjacent to the parking lot, you might be able to hang the screen over the side of the building. Get a 16-mm projector, several large speakers, a fun family movie, and a couple of cartoons.

You can then have a drive-in movie in your church parking lot. Charge admission per car or per person. You also can set up a refreshment stand and sell soft drinks, popcorn, and candy. If you're doing it in the summer, encourage people to bring chairs, chaise lounges, and so on.

Golf Club Wash. Set up a booth at the eighteenth green of a local golf course and offer to wash golf clubs for the tired hackers. All you need is permission from the golf course pro (or park board for municipal courses), a pail of soapy water, a brush, a pail of clean water, a coin collector, and a few towels. For extra money, you can wax the woods and use a metal polish on the irons. If the money is going to a worthy cause, most golfers will be glad to pay a reasonable price.

Helium Valentines. Your group can make money on Valentine's Day by selling and delivering helium balloons. Have the kids take orders three weeks prior to the holiday, then make arrangements with a local balloon or stationery store to supply you with balloons and helium at wholesale prices (or maybe even at cost). Each person ordering a balloon should fill out an order card with the name, address, and phone number of the balloon recipient, and a message for their valentine. On Valentine's Day, your group fills the balloons, attaches the messages, and delivers them.

Meal of Fortune. Place a box in the church where people can leave a card with a brief description of a special meal they would be willing to prepare and serve in their home for the highest bidder. These may be anything from enticing specialty dishes to simple grilled hamburgers. Church members can submit as many meal plans as they like, and for each they should say how many people it would serve (two, four, or whatever). They should also note whether or not children would be welcome.

Then, after a Sunday service, the meals can be auctioned off to the highest bidder without telling who will be preparing each one. After the auction, the buyer and seller agree on a convenient time to enjoy the meal together. All proceeds are collected at the time of the auction, and everything collected is profit. Best of all, this approach provides opportunities for fellowship among church members.

Super Sunday Sub Sale. A couple of weeks before the Super Bowl, put a flyer in your church bulletin announcing that your youth group is sponsoring a sub sale on Super Bowl Sunday to raise funds for your mission trip. Include the price of the subs, when to pick them up (delivery service is even better), a list of fillings available, and a tear-off coupon with space for name, address, phone number, and number of subs ordered.

Check local delis or supermarkets to see if someone will sell you sub supplies at a discount. A deli owner can also help you estimate how much you'll need for the number of subs ordered. The deli might even be wiling to prepare the materials so that your group has only to assemble them.

Besides raising money, this project builds team spirit in your youth group. You may even want to make enough extras for a Super Bowl party of your own after you're done with cleanup and delivery.

Parents' Night Out. Offer the parents and adults a night out that gives them dinner, a movie, and baby-sitting all for one low price. Movies can be rented, or you can set up a VCR and show a video.

Have the group prepare and set up for the dinner, then divide them in half. One half serves the adults while the other half feeds and cares for the kids in another room. After dinner, they switch—half the group does cleanup while the other half baby-sits. Afterward, all the youth work together to put everything away.

Macho Bake Sale. Get all the men in the church to bake cakes, cookies, and pies, and have a "Macho Bake Sale." You might even want to make it a contest between the men—no women may help them. It will be a lot of fun, generate a lot of enthusiasm, and raise good money.

(possibility of just asking the church to give)

APPENDIX C

What to Bring on a Mission Trip

General Packing List

Sleeping Bag
Good quality air mattress
Light rain gear
1 hat or cap
All necessary supplies for contact
    lenses
Extra eye glasses (if you are lost
    without them)
UV sunglasses
1 warm jacket or coat
1 sweater or sweat shirt

2 towels
1 bathing suit
Flashlight
Travel mirror
A shoulder bag or backpack
1 pack of Handi-Wipes™
Several Ziploc™ bags
Stationery
Bible
Notebook
2–3 ballpoint pens

Women's Packing List

1 good dress up outfit
4 dresses or skirt outfits
2 lightweight, cotton polo shirts and/or T-shirts
1 pair of jeans (no holes or patches, not skintight)
1 pair of cotton dress pants or culottes
Enough *marked* underwear for one week
1 nightgown or pajamas
1 lightweight housecoat
1 pair of bermuda shorts

1 pair of good shoes
1 pair of old shoes for hiking and walking
1 pair of running shoes
1 pair of flip-flops
1 pair of flat sandals
Socks for sport shoes (there is no need to bring panty hose)
Maxi pads or tampons
Basic makeup items (only)
Do not bring jewelry other than a watch and very small earrings, if you have pierced ears.

Men's Packing List

1 good dress up outfit
1 pair of lightweight dress pants
1 pair of jeans (no holes)
4 shirts (include 2–3 polo shirts)
6 T-shirts
1 pair of gym shorts
1 pair of walking shorts
Enough *marked* underwear and socks for one week
Handkerchiefs

1 pair of running shoes or sneakers (respectable condition)
1 pair of old shoes for hiking and walking
1 pair of dress shoes
1 pair of flip-flops
Shaving gear
Belt
A *small* penknife, *not* spring loaded (optional)

An Annotated List of Mission and Service Organizations

We're grateful to Adventures In Missions for their help in assembling this list of mission and service organizations. AIM is a great new resource you can use to link your group with possible mission opportunities. Using a computer data base, AIM matches the needs of your group with service opportunities both domestic and abroad. This data base can also link individuals with specific opportunities. AIM's $25.00 annual membership fee provides you with three data base reports and six issues of their *TARGET* newsletter.

Adventures in Missions
ATTN: Seth Barnes
1161 Summerwood Circle
West Palm Beach, FL 33414
(407) 790-0394

Accepts:	Junior High
	High School
	Groups
Ministries:	Construction
Time span:	One and two weeks
Mission field:	U.S., Latin America

Appalachia Service Project
Boone & Watauga Streets
Johnson City, TN 37604
(615) 928-1776

Accepts:	High School
	Groups
Ministries:	Home repair
Time span:	One week
Mission field:	Appalachia

Center for Student Missions
P.O. Box 76
San Juan Capistrano, CA 92693
(714) 248-8200

Accepts:	Junior High
	High School
	College
	Groups (limit: 25)
Ministries:	VBS
	Children's ministry
	Food distribution
	Shelter ministry
Time span:	Customized
Mission field:	Inner-city Los Angeles

Amor Ministries
7850 Golden Ave.
Lemon Grove, CA 92045
(619) 463-9800

Accepts:	High School
	College
	Individuals
Ministries:	Construction
Time span:	One week
Mission field:	Mexico

Confrontation Point Ministries
P.O. Box 50
Ozone, TN 37842
(615) 692-3999

Accepts:	Junior High
	High School
	Groups
Ministries:	Day camps
	Medical needs ministries
	Home repair
Time span:	One week
Mission field:	Appalachia

Food for the Hungry
7729 E. Greenway
Scottsdale, AZ 85260
(800) 2-HUNGER

Accepts:	High School
	College
	Groups
Ministries:	Construction
	Health services
Time span:	Two weeks
Mission field:	Worldwide

Greater Europe Mission
P.O. Box 668
Wheaton, IL 60187
(312) 426-8050

Accepts:	High School
	Individuals
Ministries:	Evangelism
	Church planting
Time span:	Nine weeks
Mission field:	Europe

Group Workcamps
P.O. Box 481
Loveland, CO 80539
(303) 669-3836

Accepts:	Junior High
	Senior High
	Groups
Ministries:	Construction
Time span:	One week
Mission field:	U.S.

Habitat for Humanity
Habitat & Church Streets
Americus, GA 31709-3498
(912) 925-6935

Accepts:	High School
	College
	Groups
Ministries:	Construction
Time span:	One week
Mission field:	U.S. (also has longer-term
	ministries worldwide)

Inner City Impact
ATTN: Bill Dillon
2704 W. North Ave.
Chicago, IL 60647
(312) 384-4200

Accepts:	High School
	Groups
Ministries:	Backyard clubs
	Evangelism
	Construction
Time span:	One week
Mission field:	Inner-city Chicago

Institute of Outreach Ministries
Azusa Pacific University
Azusa, CA 91702
(818) 969-3434

Accepts:	Junior High
	High School
	Singles
	Groups
Ministries:	VBS
	Children's ministry
	Evangelism
Time span:	One week
Mission field:	Mexico

International Teams
ATTN: Rick Knox
P.O. Box 203
Prospect Heights, IL 60070
(312) 870-3800

Accepts:	College
	Individuals
Ministries:	Evangelism
	Church planting

	Physical needs
Time span:	Three months to two years
Mission field:	Worldwide

John Perkins Foundation
ATTN: Debbie Perkins
1581 Navarro Ave.
Pasadena, CA 91103
(818) 791-7439

Accepts:	High School
	Groups
	Individuals
Ministries:	Physical needs
	Evangelism
	Children's ministry
Time span:	Three days to one week
Mission field:	Pasadena, CA

Latin American Mission
P.O. Box 52-7900
Miami, FL 33152-8400
(305) 884-8400

Accepts:	High School
	College
	Groups
	Individuals
Ministries:	Camps
	VBS
	Construction
Time span:	One and two weeks
Mission field:	Latin America

Mennonite Board of Missions
P.O. Box 370
Elkhart, IN 46515-0370
(219) 294-7523

Accepts:	Junior High
	High School
	Groups
Ministries:	Construction
Time span:	One week
Mission field:	U.S.

Missions Outreach Inc.
P.O. Box 73
Bethany, MO 64424
(816) 425-2277

Accepts:	High School
	Individuals
Ministries:	Evangelism
	Construction
Time span:	Seven weeks
Mission field:	Worldwide

Mountain T.O.P.
P.O. Box 128
Altamont, TN 37301
(615) 692-3999

Accepts:	Junior High
	High School
	Groups
Ministries:	Construction
Time span:	One week
Mission field:	Tennessee

Project Serve*
P.O. Box 419
Wheaton, IL 60189
(708) 668-6600

Accepts:	High School
	Groups
	Individuals

Ministries: Construction
 VBS
 Evangelism
Time span: Two weeks
Mission field: Mexico
* Project Serve is an independent organization and is not affiliated with the Project Serve trips I led while at the Wheaton Bible Church.

SIMA/Mission to the World
P.O. Box 29765
Atlanta, GA 30359
(404) 320-6090
Accepts: Junior High
 High School
 Groups
Ministries: Construction
 VBS
 Evangelism
Time span: Two weeks
Mission field: Worldwide

Spectrum Ministries
3286 Erie Street
San Diego, CA 92117
(619) 276-1963
Accepts: High School
 College
 Groups
Ministries: Children's ministry
 Physical needs
 Construction
 Food distribution
Time span: Customized
Mission field: Mexico

Teen Missions International
P.O. Box 1056
Merritt Island, FL 32952-1056
(407) 453-0350
Accepts: High School
 College
 Individuals
Ministries: Construction
 VBS
 Evangelism
Time span: Nine weeks
Mission field: Worldwide

Voice of Calvary Ministries
P.O. Box 10562
Jackson, MS 39289-0562
(601) 353-1635
Accepts: High School
 Groups
Ministries: Construction
Time span: One week
Mission field: Mississippi

Work & Witness/Nazarene Church
P.O. Box 12295
Albuquerque, NM 87195
(505) 877-0240
Accepts: Junior High
 High School
 Groups
Ministries: Evangelism
 VBS
Time span: One week
Mission field: U.S.

World Servants
8233 Gator Lane, #6
West Palm Beach, FL 33411
(407) 790-0800

Accepts:	High School
	Groups
Ministries:	Construction
	VBS
	Evangelism
Time span:	One week
Mission field:	U.S.

Youth Unlimited Gospel Outreach
P.O. Box 22457
San Dimas, CA 91773
(714) 592-6621

Accepts:	High School
	Groups
Ministries:	Construction
	VBS
	Evangelism
Time span:	One week
Mission field:	Mexico

Youth With A Mission
P.O. Box 22457
Denver, CO 80222

Accepts:	High School
	College
	Groups
	Individuals
Ministries:	Evangelism
	Children's ministry
Time span:	One, two, and three weeks
Mission field:	Worldwide